Macmillan English

Language Book

4

Mary Bowen
Louis Fidge
Liz Hocking
Wendy Wren

Scope and sequence: Units 1-9

	Theme	LANGUAGE BOOK 4		
		Reading and understanding	Vocabulary	Language building
Unit 1	Fire	stimulus: *The Sun and the Wind* text type: play comprehension: multiple choice/extension	short words in longer words	revision – nouns/proper nouns/adjectives/adverbs
Unit 2	Fire	stimulus: *Volcanoes* text type: information/explanation comprehension: ordering steps in the explanation/extension	words and definitions/riddle	plural – **o** words
Unit 3	Food	stimulus: *Clever Polly* text type: short story comprehension: Who said it?/extension	What can you do? What can you eat?/homophones	direct speech
Unit 4	Food	stimulus: *Restaurants and recipes* text type: lists and instructions comprehension: true or false	food words/alphabetical order	proper nouns
		REVISION: UNITS 1-4		
Unit 5	Journeys	stimulus: *Journey to Jo'burg* text type: modern fiction - extract comprehension: cloze/extension	adjectives/alphabetical order	noun-verb agreement
Unit 6	Journeys	stimulus: *A long journey* text type: letter comprehension: true or false/extension	rhymes/codes	comparative/superlative **er/est** and irregulars
Unit 7	Animals	stimulus: *The ant and the beetle* text type: fable comprehension: multiple choice/extension	synonyms	comparative/superlative with more/most
Unit 8	Animals	stimulus: *An animal dictionary/An animal encyclopaedia* text type: alphabetical texts comprehension: literal – words and definitions/extension	alphabetical order – words in a dictionary	possessive nouns – singular
Unit 9	Animals	stimulus: *Lions/The 'Veggy' Lion* text type: poetry comprehension: literal/extension	collective nouns	statements and questions
		REVISION: UNITS 5-9		

LANGUAGE BOOK 4	FLUENCY BOOK 4	LANGUAGE BOOK 4		
Grammar	**Fluency**	**Spelling**	**Writing**	**Reading extension**
past simple - irregular verbs *The wind blew the trees.* *The sun shone on the grass.* *The grass caught fire.*	1 *Holiday clothes for different weather*	**ey** words	the next scene of the play	*The Great Fire of London*
past continuous *The volcano was sleeping.* *The next day it was grumbling* *People were running from their homes.*	2 *Forest fires* *Fire fighting in Australia*	**ire** words	information writing on Vesuvius	*When there's a Fire in the jungle/The Sun* (fire poems)
past continuous and past simple *While Polly was cooking, the doorbell rang.* *While Billy was running, he fell over.*	3 *Sea life* *Sea creature food chain*	**le** words	dialogue	*Why do we eat?*
infinitive of purpose *They went to the restaurant to have a meal.* *She bought some vegetables to make soup.*	4 *The Let's go! Club Café* *Café snacks*	**ar** words	instructions	*Fascinating food facts*
	REVISION: UNITS 1-4			
modal verb **should** *I should take you back home.* *You should not be walking alone.*	5 *Wheels* *Moving with wheels*	**dge** words	characters in stories	*Soraya's blanket*
will to express the future *I will write again soon.* *She will not visit London.*	6 *South African journey* *South Africa; travelling by plane*	soft **g** words	letter	*How people learnt to fly*
pronouns *Someone has to get food.* *Can anybody help me?* *The beetle did not have anything to eat.* *There was nothing to eat in the fields.*	7 *The lazy mouse* *Re-telling a story with a moral*	silent **k** and **w** words	story structure	*All about ants*
few/fewer/the fewest; little/less/the least *There are few pandas in zoo A. (fewer pandas; the fewest pandas)* *There is a little food for the animals. (less food; the least food)*	8 *Animals in danger* *Endangered animals*	silent **b** words	dictionaries – words and definitions	*Animal fun – 2 poems: Teaser* (riddle)/*Undersea tea* (very simple shape poem)
question words *Who wrote the poem?* *Where do they live?* *(What? How? Why? Which? When? How much? How many?)*	9 *South African safari*	syllables – one- and two-syllable words	rhymes	*The last laugh*
	REVISION: UNITS 5-9			

Scope and sequence: Units 10-18

	Theme	LANGUAGE BOOK 4		
		Reading and understanding	Vocabulary	Language building
Unit 10	Celebration	stimulus: *Open Day* text type: play comprehension: multiple choice/extension	dictionary work – word meanings and spellings	irregular plurals
Unit 11	Celebration	stimulus: *Celebrating success – Amy Johnson* text type: biography comprehension: sequencing/extension	compound words	adverbs of time
Unit 12	Weather	stimulus: *The flying house* (extract from *The Wizard of Oz*) text type: narrative fantasy adventure comprehension: true or false/extension	thesaurus work – synonyms	direct speech (split sentences)
Unit 13	Weather	stimulus: *Hurricane Harry* text type: newspaper report comprehension: cloze procedure/extension	categorising/classifying thematic weather words	reported speech
		REVISION: UNITS 10-13		
Unit 14	Sport	stimulus: *It's a knock-out!* (football story) text type: story with familiar setting comprehension: Who said it?/extension	homonyms	adverbs of place
Unit 15	Sport	stimulus: *The Olympic Games* text type: information text with chart comprehension: reading a chart/extension	alphabetical order according to 1st, 2nd and 3rd letters	subject and object
Unit 16	Relationships	stimulus: *The Martian and the Supermarket* text type: fantasy adventure comprehension: sentence completion/extension	overused words: said – suggesting alternatives	possessive adjectives
Unit 17	Relationships	stimulus: *The visit* text type: recount comprehension: sequencing/extension	thesaurus work – synonyms and antonyms	apostrophes of possession (plural)
Unit 18	Relationships	stimulus: *What is a friend?* text type: poetry (including an acrostic poem) comprehension: literal questions/extension	rhyming words	possessive pronouns
		REVISION: UNITS 14-18		

	LANGUAGE BOOK 4	FLUENCY BOOK 4	LANGUAGE BOOK 4		
	Grammar	**Fluency**	**Spelling**	**Writing**	**Reading extension**
	first conditional *If you help me, we will make soup together.* *We will make vegetable soup if you bring different vegetables.*	10 *Welcome back!* Party food	prefix **re**	continuing the playscript	*Matiwara's and the Old Woman* (traditional African story)
	question tags *He is a pilot, isn't he?* *Planes are fast aren't they?* *You are learning to fly aren't you?*	11 *Bravery awards* Brave actions; computer games	soft **c**	writing a biography (using notes)	*Celebrating the sunshine!* (poem)
	too + adjective; adjective + **enough** *The wind was too strong.* *The house was not strong enough.*	12 *Hollywood and favourite films*	silent letters within words	descriptive writing (describing a setting)	*The weather forecast* (weather symbols and descriptions)
	present perfect *The wind has blown the roof off.* *Have you ever seen such devastation?* *I have never seen anything like it.*	13 *Caribbean adventure* The Caribbean and music	**-or** suffix	writing own newspaper report	*Wind* (poem)
	REVISION: UNITS 10–13				
	present perfect with **yet** and **just** *Have you finished with it yet?* *I have not finished with it yet.* *I have just started.*	14 *Extreme sports*	two-syllable words with medial double consonants	planning and writing story sequel	*Fascinating football facts*
	exclamations with **What** (a/an) *What a wonderful stadium!* *What huge crowds!* *What excitement!*	15 *Sports champions* Favourite sports	**o** sounds like **u** (nothing)	information in chart form	*Dawn Fraser* (biography)
	making offers and suggestions *Would you like some help?* *How/What about having a picnic?* *Shall we try it?* *Let's buy some grapes.*	16 *The solar system* The planets	three-syllable words	using dialogue/ continuing story	*The professor and the ferryman* (story with a moral)
	gerunds *We enjoyed visiting the zoo.* *The chimpanzees were good at climbing.* *We were interested in watching the animals.*	17 *Zoo vets* Zoos; zoo vets and nurses	**al** as prefix and suffix	recount (from personal experience)	*Endangered animals* (factual information)
	relative clauses with **who** *A pilot is someone who flies planes.* *A nurse is someone who works in a hospital.*	18 *The big quiz*	**el** words	acrostic poems	*The world with its countries* (poem)
	REVISION: UNITS 14–18				

Some characters you will meet in this book

This is **Wordsworth**. He knows a lot about words. He will help you with vocabulary activities.

Bernie the builder will help you with grammar. He will help you to build sentences correctly.

Captain Superspell is a great speller. She will be there to help you with spelling. She will teach you helpful spelling rules.

Penny Pen loves writing. She loves helping people, too. Penny is always around to help you with writing activities.

The Sun and the Wind

The Sun and the Wind are always arguing. The Sun thinks he is stronger than the Wind. The Wind thinks he is stronger than the Sun.

Scene 1

Setting	In the sky
Characters	The Sun, the Wind, the Cloud, the Man

The Sun and the Wind often argued. The Sun thought he was stronger than the Wind. The Wind thought he was stronger than the Sun. One day they met in the sky. The little Cloud was near them.

The Wind:	I'm very strong. I'm stronger than the rain. I'm stronger than the snow. I'm stronger than you!
The Sun:	I'm very strong. I'm stronger than the rain. I'm stronger than the snow. I'm stronger than you!
The Wind:	No, you are not!
The Sun:	Yes, I am!
The Wind:	I can blow and blow. Yesterday, I blew the trees and made them fall over. I blew the clouds and made them move.
The Sun:	I'm made of fire. I can burn and burn. Yesterday, I shone on the dry grass and it caught fire. I shone on the water in the river and it dried up.
The Cloud:	You are always arguing! I've got an idea. We can see who is stronger. We can have a test.
The Wind:	A test? What do you mean?
The Cloud:	There's a Man walking in the valley. He's wearing a heavy coat. Let's see who can make the Man take off his coat.
The Wind:	I can do that.
The Sun:	I can do that.

Scene 2

Setting	In a valley
Characters	The Wind, the Sun, the Man

The Man is walking in the valley. The Cloud tells the Wind to try first.

The Wind:　I'm going to blow and blow. I'm going to blow off the Man's coat.

The Wind blew and blew.

The Man:　It's very windy! I must hold on to my coat.

The Wind:　I must blow harder. The Man is holding on to his coat.

The Wind blew and blew but the Man held on to his coat.

The Wind:　I'm very tired. I cannot blow any more.

Now it was the Sun's turn.

The Sun:　I'm going to use my fire and shine and shine.

The Man:　It's getting hotter and hotter.

The Sun:　Look! The Man is getting hot.

The Man:　I'm very hot. I must take off my coat.

The Sun:　Look! The Man is taking off his coat. My fire made the Man take off his coat. I win! I am stronger than the Wind.

9

Comprehension

1 Look back. Find the correct answers. Circle them.

1 The Wind thought it was stronger than	(a) the rain.	b the cloud.
2 The Sun burnt	a the trees.	b the grass.
3 The Man was wearing	a a coat.	b a jumper.
4 When the Wind blew, the Man	a took off his coat.	b held on to his coat.
5 When the Sun shone, the Man	a took off his coat.	b held on to his coat.

2 Discuss your answers to these questions.

1 Why does the Wind think it is stronger than the Sun?
2 Why does the Sun think it is stronger than the Wind?
3 The Cloud wants to stop them arguing. What is his idea?
4 Do you think the Cloud's idea was a good one? Why? Why not?
5 How do you think the Wind felt when the Man took off his coat?

Vocabulary

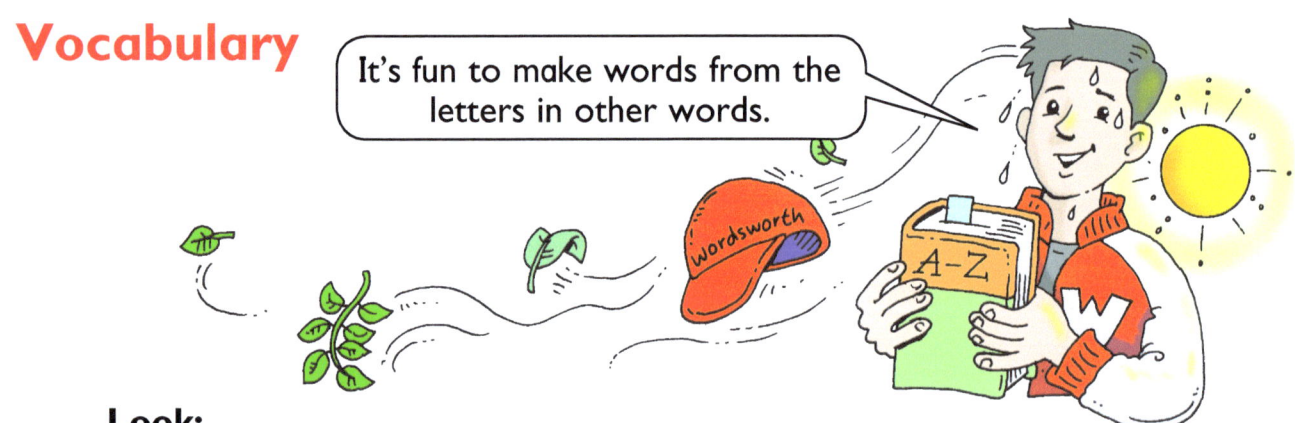

It's fun to make words from the letters in other words.

Look:

y **e** s t **e** r d a y   -   **yes**   y e s t e r **d** **a** **y**   -   **day**

y e **s** **t** e r d **a** **y**   -   **stay**   y e s **t** e r d **a** **t** **e**   -   **date**

1 Make three words from:

1 s t r o n g e r   _strong_   _____   _____
2 w e a r i n g   _____   _____   _____
3 h a r d e r   _____   _____   _____

Language building

Remember!
A **noun** is a **naming word**.

A **proper noun** is a **special** naming word. It begins with a **capital letter**.

 a tree

 Ben

1 Write the *proper nouns* with *capital letters*.

> penny   coat   wednesday   valley
> bernie   wordsworth   grass   july

 There are five proper nouns to find.

Penny   _____   _____   _____   _____

Remember!
An **adjective** tells us more about a **noun**.

the grass — noun

the **dry** grass — adjective noun

2 Write the *adjective*.

1 The orange sun came up in the morning.   _orange_
2 The long grass moved in the wind.   _____
3 I can see a dark cloud.   _____
4 The man is wearing a heavy coat.   _____
5 A cloud covered the hot sun.   _____

Remember!
Adverbs tell us more about verbs.
They tell us 'how' something was done.

I must blow **harder**.

3 Use these *adverbs* in sentences.
Write in your copy book.

> quickly   brightly   slowly

Grammar

Do you remember the play about the Sun and the Wind?

Yesterday, the Wind **blew** the trees.
It **made** the trees fall over.

Yesterday, the Sun **shone** on the grass.
The grass **caught** fire.

1 **Write the *past* tense.**

1 make   made   2 have _____   3 take _____
4 hold   _____   5 shine _____   6 catch _____
5 blow   _____   8 see   _____   9 burn _____

Check in the word snake. Were you right?

burntshoneblewmadesawcaughttheldtookhad

2 **Ask and answer.**

Choose from these verbs: | catch   fall   blow   have   see   burn |

1 wind – trees   Did the Wind blow the trees?   Yes, it did. or No, it didn't.

2 trees – over   3 Sun – grass   4 grass – fire
5 Cloud – Man   6 Man – thin coat   7 Wind – softly

3 **Are these sentences true or false? Circle.**

1 The Wind blew a house over.   true   false
2 The Sun burnt a forest.   true   false
3 They saw a woman in the valley.   true   false
4 The Man had a heavy coat.   true   false
5 The Man held on to his hat.   true   false

Correct the false sentences. Say, then write in your copy book.
Like this: The Wind did not ...

Turn to Fluency Book 4 Programme 1.

Grammar   past simple of irregular verbs

Spelling

Some words end in **ey** which makes a sound like **ee**.

vall**ey** k**ey**

1 **Complete the words with *ey*.**

1  turk**e y**

2  monk__ __

3  chimn__ __

4  jock__ __

Read the words. Discuss what they mean.

2 **Write *ey* words. Read the words.**

1 We spend this. __ __ __ __ __

2 Bees make this. __ __ __ __ __

3 This animal looks like a horse. __ __ __ __ __ __

3 **Choose three *ey* words from this page.
Make a sentence about each word. Write in your copy book.**

Like this: *I lost my k**ey** in the river.*

Spelling *ey words*

Class writing

Write the next scene of the play.
- The Wind is very angry. It wants to try again.
- The Sun says it will try again.
- The Cloud sees the Woman wearing a hat.

What will happen in your scene?
- Can the Wind blow off the Woman's hat?
- Can the Sun make the Woman take off her hat?

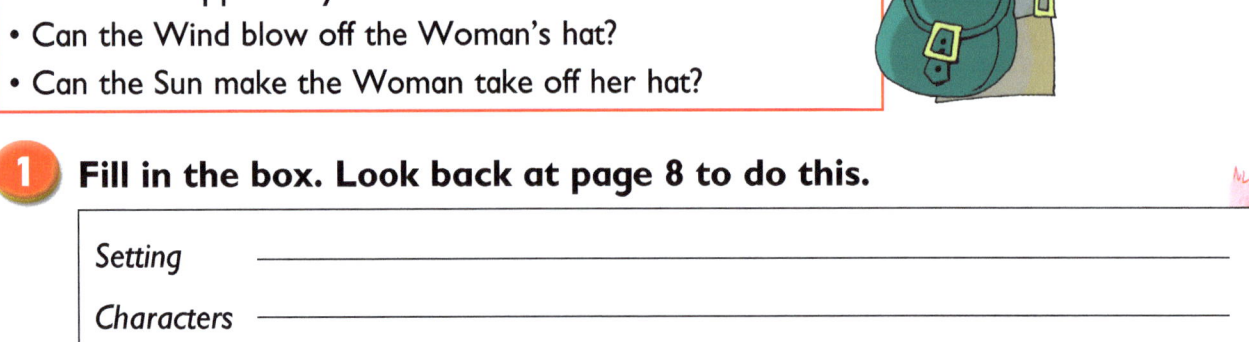

1 **Fill in the box. Look back at page 8 to do this.**

   Setting _____
   Characters _____

2 **What are the characters doing at the start of the scene?**

_____
_____
_____

3 **What do the characters say?**

Character	What the character says
The Wind	Let's try again. I can make the Woman take off her hat.
The Sun	_____
_____	_____
_____	_____
_____	_____
_____	_____

Finish the scene in your copy book.

Reading for enrichment

The Great Fire of London

A long time ago, a lot of houses in London were made of wood. There were many wooden houses close together in small streets. A lot of the wooden houses had thatched roofs. One of the small streets was called Pudding Lane. In Pudding Lane, Mr Farynor had a baker's shop. On 2 September 1666, the Great Fire of London started in Mr Farynor's shop.

A spark from the bakery fire lit some hay in the yard. It was early in the morning and only a few people were awake. No one saw the fire until houses near the baker's shop were burning. The fire reached a building full of oil and candles. The building, the candles and the oil burnt. No one could stop the fire.

Men tried to put out the fire with buckets of water but it did not work. The fire got to London Bridge. It burnt all the wooden houses on the bridge.

The Great Fire did not stop for five days. It burnt London Bridge, 13,000 houses and 97 churches. Nine people died.

In the end, men filled some houses with gunpowder. They blew up the houses to make an empty space. The fire could not cross the empty space and so it stopped.

Reading extension — historical information text

Volcanoes

Most mountains take millions of years to grow big and high like the ones we see today. However, some mountains can grow in a few weeks! These mountains are called volcanoes.

Long ago, when the Earth was young, there were thousands of volcanoes. They poured out fire, smoke and lava. Now there are fewer than 500 active volcanoes. The rest are dormant, which means 'sleeping'.

Volcanoes start to grow when there is a very deep crack, or vent, in the Earth. Hot, molten rock, called magma, moves up from deep inside the Earth and pours out of the vent. When it pours out of the vent, it is called lava. The hot lava cools and goes hard. The hard lava blocks the vent for a few days, weeks, months, or years. It stops the lava pouring out.

When a lot more hot magma moves up, it pushes the hard lava away. The volcano erupts again. Hot lava, smoke and ash explode out of the vent at the top.

Sometimes dormant volcanoes erupt suddenly. Volcanoes that erupt suddenly can kill people and animals.

Look at this diagram of a volcano.

Information books often use diagrams to help you understand.

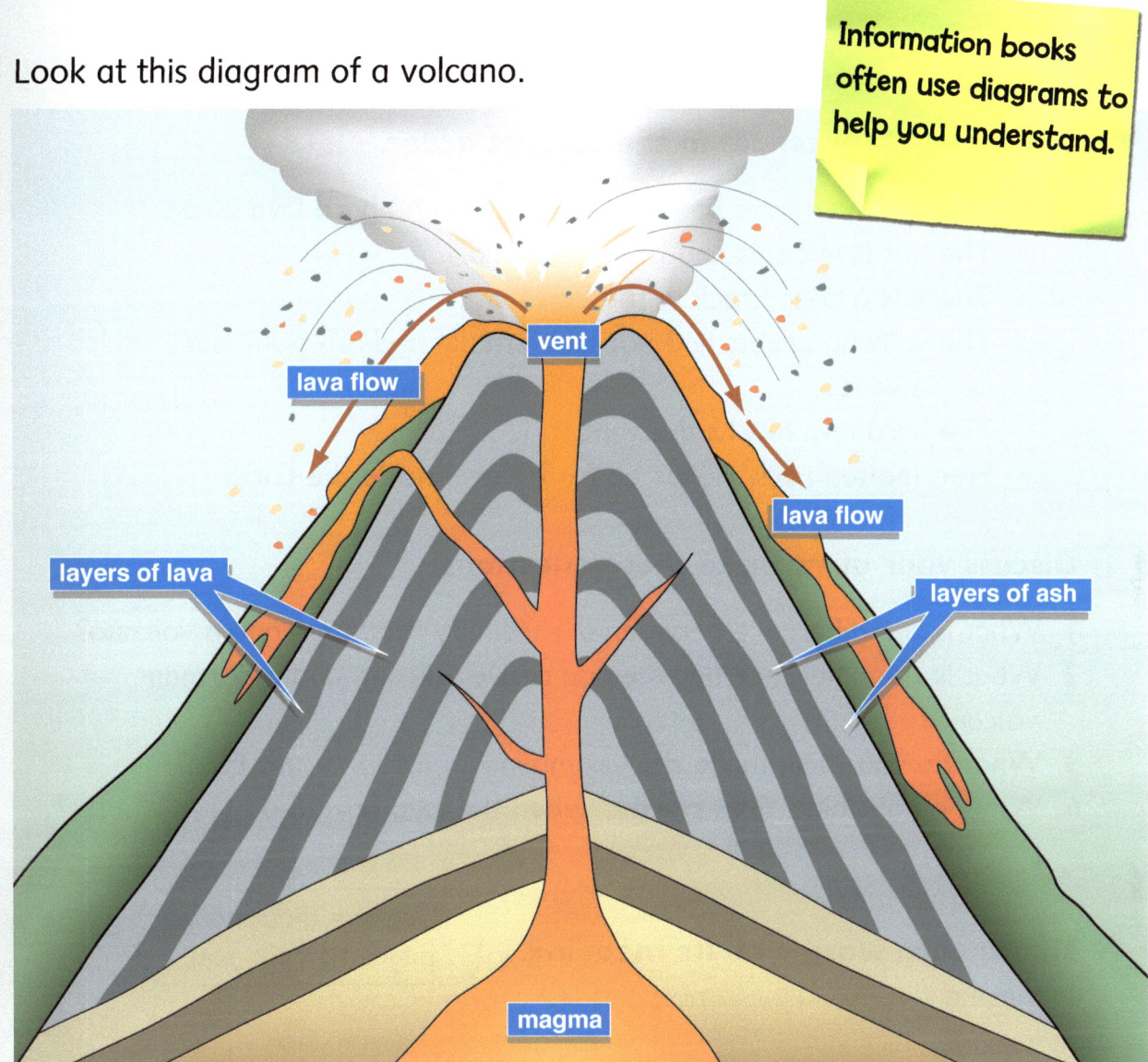

Etna erupts!

On Saturday 26th October 2002, Mount Etna was sleeping quietly. The next day the volcano was grumbling. Then, on Tuesday 29th October, it erupted. One thousand people left their homes and the lava damaged a hundred houses. As the lava was flowing down the mountain, fires started. Europe's most active volcano was throwing lava a hundred metres into the air. This was the fourth big eruption of Mount Etna in the last 309 years!

Comprehension

1 **Number the sentences in the correct order.**

___ The magma moves up again and pushes the hard lava away.
___ The hot lava cools and becomes hard.
_1_ There is a deep crack in the Earth.
___ The volcano erupts and hot lava, smoke and ash pour out of the vent.
___ The hard lava blocks the vent.
___ Hot, molten rock moves up from deep inside the Earth.

2 **Discuss your answers to these questions.**

1 What is the difference between an ordinary mountain and a volcano?
2 What is the difference between an active volcano and a dormant volcano?
3 What do you think made the 'grumbling' noise in Mount Etna?
4 Why do you think 'fires started' when the lava flowed down the sides?

Vocabulary

1 **Match each word with its meaning.**

Use the dictionary pages to help you.

1 magma ___
2 lava ___
3 vent ___
4 erupts ___

a explodes
b hole in the top of a volcano
c hot, liquid rock inside the Earth
d hot, liquid rock flowing out of a volcano

2 **What am I?**

Write the letter here.

Can you guess what I am?

My first is in VENT but not in TENT   _v_
My second is in BONE but not in BENT   ___
My third is in WALK but not in WAKE   ___
My fourth is in CAKE but not in BAKE   ___
My fifth is in SAT but not in SET   ___
My sixth is in NOT but not in LOT   ___
My seventh is in LOSS but not in LESS   ___

Language building

> **Remember!**
> • **singular** means **one**.   • **plural** means **more than one**.
>
>  a volcano     two volcano**es**
>
> For most nouns ending in **o** we add **es** to make them plural.

1 **Write the *plurals*. Read the *plurals*.**

1 tomato _tomatoes_   2 potato _____   3 volcano _____

4  hero _____   5  domino _____   6  flamingo _____

> For nouns to do with **music** we just add **s**.
>
> For nouns ending in **oo** we just add **s**.
>
> two piano**s**
>
> three cockatoo**s**
>
>

2 **Write the *plurals*. Read the *plurals*.**

1 piccolo  _piccolos_   2 kangaroo  _____

3 bamboo  _____   4 cello  _____

3 **Learn these *plurals*. They do not follow the rules!**

photos   videos   hippos

4 **Write a sentence using each word. Write in your copy book.**

Language building   *plural - o words*   19

Grammar

What do you remember about Mount Etna?

On 26th October 2002, Mount Etna **was sleeping**. The next day, it **was grumbling**.

Two days later, the volcano **was throwing** lava into the air.
Soon the lava **was flowing** down the mountain.

1 **Find the correct ending.**

1 On 26th October Mount Etna __d__   a was erupting.
2 The next day it ____   b were running from their homes.
3 By 29th October it ____   c was flowing down the mountain.
4 Soon lava ____   d was sleeping quietly.
5 Frightened people ____   e was grumbling.

2 **Look and talk.**

What was happening when the photographer took the pictures?

3 **Listen, then talk.**

1 Shut your eyes and listen for a moment or two.
2 Open your eyes.
3 What could you hear when your eyes were closed?

Turn to Fluency Book 4 Programme 2.

Grammar   past continuous

Spelling

A few words end with the letters **ire**.

 f**ire**

1 Do these word sums. Read the words.

1 　　w　+　ire　=　_____

2 　　f　+　ire　=　_____

3 　　ump　+　ire　=　_____

2 Choose and complete.　　　　fire　wire　tired

1 He was _____ after his long walk.
2 The _____ made the room very warm.
3 There was a _____ at the back of the computer.

3 Write the meanings. Use the dictionary pages.

to tire _____
a tyre _____

Spelling　**ire** words

Class writing

Here is a Fact File about a famous volcano called Vesuvius.

Vesuvius

Country: Italy
Nearby towns: Naples, Pompeii, Herculaneum
Height: 1,220 metres
Erupted: 24th August, AD 79
Result: Pompeii and Herculaneum disappeared under ash and lava.
How do we know? A man called Pliny wrote about the volcano when it erupted in AD 79.

1 Look at the information writing about Etna on page 17.

2 Write answers. Use the Fact File about Vesuvius.

- Where is Vesuvius?
- How high is it?
- What happened to the towns?
- What towns is it near?
- When did it erupt?
- How do we know about it?

Writing — information writing on Vesuvius

Reading for enrichment

Fire poems

When there's a Fire in the Jungle

When there's a fire in the jungle,
They call the Elephant Brigade,
Who race with their trunks full of water,
To the place that has to be sprayed.
But if the fire is a big one,
It happens as often as not,
That the elephants drink all the water,
To stop themselves getting too hot.

Martin Honeysett

The Sun

The sun
Is round
Like a bun
And burning hot,
Hotter than any teapot:
It is a ball of flames.

Julie Edwards

Reading extension — fire poems

Clever Polly

One day, while Polly was cooking, the doorbell rang. Polly opened the door. There was a great, black wolf!

He put his foot inside the door and said, 'I'm going to eat you!'

'Oh no,' said Polly. 'I don't want you to eat me.'

'Oh, yes,' said the wolf, 'I'm going to eat you. But first, tell me, what is that delicious smell?'

'Come to the kitchen,' said Polly, 'and I'll show you.'

She took the wolf to the kitchen. There, on the table, was a delicious-looking pie.

'Have a slice,' said Polly.

The wolf was hungry and he said, 'Yes, please!' Polly cut a big piece for him. When he had eaten it, the wolf asked for another slice, and then for another.

'Now,' said Polly after the third helping, 'are you going to eat me?'

'Sorry. I'm too full of pie,' said the wolf. 'I'll come back another day to eat you.'

A week later, Polly was in her house again, and again the doorbell rang. Polly opened the door. There was the wolf again.

'This time I'm going to eat you, Polly,' said the wolf.

'All right,' said Polly, 'but first, can you smell this?'

The wolf put his nose inside the door. 'Delicious!' he said. 'What is it?'

'Come and see,' said Polly.

In the kitchen was a large chocolate cake.

'Have a slice,' said Polly.

'Yes, please!' said the wolf greedily. He ate six big slices.

'Now, are you going to eat me?' asked Polly.

'Sorry,' said the wolf, 'I'm too full of cake. I'll come back.' He slunk out of the back door.

A week later, the doorbell rang again. Polly opened the door, and there was the wolf.

'This time you can't escape!' he snarled. 'I'm going to eat you now!'

'Smell in here first,' said Polly.

'Marvellous!' said the wolf. 'What is it?'

'Toffee,' said Polly. 'But aren't you going to eat me?'

'Couldn't I have a tiny bit of toffee, first?' asked the wolf. 'It's my favourite food.'

'Come to the kitchen,' said Polly.

In the kitchen, the toffee was cooking on the stove. 'I must have a taste,' said the wolf.

'It's hot,' said Polly.

But the wolf took the spoon out of the saucepan and put it in his mouth. 'OW HOWL! OW!'

It was so hot that it burnt his tongue. It was so sticky that it stuck to his mouth. The wolf howled. Then he ran out of the house and *never came back*!

Comprehension

1 Who said it?

1 'I'm going to eat you now!' wolf
2 'Have a slice.' _____
3 'Now, are you going to eat me?' _____
4 'I'm too full of pie.' _____
5 'Delicious!' _____
6 'I'll come back.' _____
7 'What is it?' _____
8 'It's hot.' _____

2 Discuss your answers to these questions.

1 What did the wolf eat the first time he was in Polly's kitchen?
2 What did the wolf eat the second time he was in Polly's kitchen?
3 Why do you think Polly fed the wolf?
4 Why do you think Polly made toffee?
5 Do you think Polly was clever? Why?/Why not?

Vocabulary

1 Sort the words.

These words are in the story.

> run   pie   ask
> cake   tell   toffee

Things you can eat: _____   _____   _____
Things you can do: _____   _____   _____

2 Find the difference. Write the meanings in your copy books.

1 no   know
2 to   too
3 right   write
4 see   sea
5 so   sew

These words are called **homophones**.
They **sound the same**.
They have **different meanings**.
Use the **Dictionary** pages to help you.

Language building

> **Direct speech** is when we write the **exact words** someone said.
>
> 'I'm going to eat you, now!' said the wolf.
>
> If the same person goes on speaking, we:
> • write new speech marks
> • use a capital letter
> • *do not* begin a new line.
>
> 'Oh, no,' said Polly. 'I don't want you to eat me.'

1 **This *direct speech* is split into *two parts*. Change it to *one part*.**

1 'Oh, yes,' said the wolf. 'I'm going to eat you.'

' <u>Oh, yes, I'm going to eat you</u> ,' said the wolf.

2 'I'm too full of pie,' said the wolf. 'I'll come back another day.'

' _____ ,' said the wolf.

3 'It's a chocolate cake,' said Polly. 'Have a slice.'

' _____ ,' said Polly.

4 'I'm too full of cake,' said the wolf. 'I'll come back.'

' _____ ,' said the wolf.

5 'Toffee is my favourite food,' said the wolf. 'I must have a taste.'

' _____ ,' said the wolf.

2 **Discuss how to split this *direct speech* into *two parts*.**

1 'I've just finished my book. It was very good,' said Ben.
2 'I've read that one. I didn't like it,' said Tom.
3 'What are you reading now? Is it good?' asked Ben.
4 'I'm reading *Clever Polly*. I think it's great,' said Tom.

Grammar

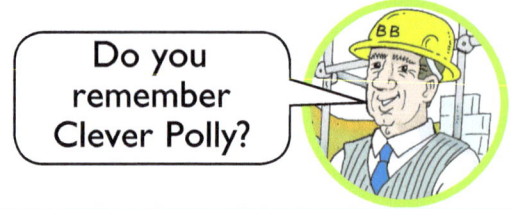

Do you remember Clever Polly?

While Polly **was cooking**, the doorbell **rang**.

While Polly **was making** a cake, the wolf **came** to her house.

While Polly **was working** in the kitchen, the wolf **arrived**.

1 Look at the pictures and finish the sentences.

1 While Polly was making a cake, ____

2 While the wolf was walking home, ____

3 While the boys were playing football, ____

4 While we were watching, ____

a it started to rain.
b the telephone rang.
c the volcano erupted.
d Bobby fell over.

Be careful! Put the verbs in the correct tense.

2 Complete the sentences with the verbs.

1 (cook, come) While Polly <u>was cooking</u>, the wolf _____.
2 (run, fall) While Bill _____,
   he _____ over.
3 (swim, see) While they _____,
   they _____ a dolphin.
4 (write, make) While I _____,
   I _____ a mistake.

Turn to Fluency Book 4 Programme 3.

28   Grammar   *while + past continuous; past simple*

Spelling

The letters **le** sometimes come at the **end** of a word.

tab**le**

1 Complete each word with *le*. Write the words.

1 cand l e
   candle

2 crad ___ ___
   _____

3 kett ___ ___
   _____

4 ratt ___ ___
   _____

5 need ___ ___
   _____

6 triang ___ ___
   _____

Read the words. Discuss what they mean.

2 Sort the letters then write the words.

1 betla

table

2 leeend

_____

3 darlec
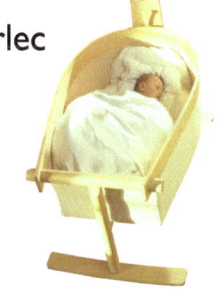
_____

4 lanced

_____

5 graintel

_____

6 tektel

_____

Reading for enrichment

Why do we eat?

We eat to stay healthy.
Different foods help us in different ways.

Foods	Why we need them
bread pasta cereals rice  	These foods have starch in them. They give us energy.
biscuits cakes sweets 	These foods have sugar in them. They give us energy.
fish meat milk eggs 	These foods help the body to get better when we are sick or hurt.
cheese butter cooking oil 	These foods have fat in them. They give us energy.
fruit vegetables 	These foods are full of vitamins. They keep us healthy.
water 	Seventy per cent of your body is water. Drink a lot of water every day.

Reading extension   information chart: food and health

unit 4

Restaurants and recipes

It was Harry's birthday. He was very excited. Harry and his family went to a restaurant to have a birthday meal. Here is the menu.

Green Park Restaurant

Starters
Melon

Vegetable Soup and bread

Main course
Roast Chicken

Lamb Surprise

Tomato Pizza

Big Beef Burger

All served with:

Carrots, Peas *or* Salad

French Fries *or* Party Potato Nests

Desserts
Banana Split

Ice Cream

Pineapple Pyramid

Fruit Salad

Chocolate Cake

Stimulus — lists and instructions

Party Potato Nests

This recipe makes 8 party potato nests.

> Harry had Vegetable Soup as a starter. He had Lamb Surprise and Party Potato Nests for his main course. He had Pineapple Pyramid with Ice Cream for dessert. He liked the Party Potato Nests a lot. They were delicious. This is how you make them.

You need:
675g peeled potatoes   75g cheese
25g butter   8 small tomatoes
$\frac{1}{4}$ teaspoon black pepper   2 tablespoons fresh, chopped parsley

Instructions:

1

Cook the potatoes in boiling water for 10 minutes.

2

Drain the potatoes.

3

Mash the potatoes with the butter and black pepper.

4

Stir in 50g of the cheese. Leave it to cool.

5

Shape the potato mixture into 8 small nests.

6

Put them on an oiled baking tray.

7

Chop the tomatoes.

8

Put some chopped tomato on each potato nest.

9

Sprinkle with parsley and cheese.

10

Cook under a medium grill for 8 to 10 minutes. Serve immediately.

Comprehension

1 **Write *true* or *false*.**

Look at the menu.
1. You can have roast chicken as a starter. _false_
2. Tomato pizza is a dessert. _____
3. You can have ice cream for dessert. _____

Look at the recipe.
4. You need 25 grams of butter. _____
5. You do not need tomatoes. _____
6. You mash the potatoes with the cheese. _____

2 **Discuss your answers to these questions.**

1. What did Harry have for his birthday meal?
2. What would you choose from the menu?
3. What does it mean when it says 'Drain the potatoes'?
4. Why should you put the potato nests on 'an oiled baking tray'?
5. Would you like to eat Party Potato Nests? Why? Why not?

Vocabulary

These words are things you can eat.

1 **Label the food.**

pizza   _____   _____

_____   _____   _____

2 **Write the food words in alphabetical order.**

1. _banana_   2. _____   3. _____
4. _____   5. _____   6. _____

Language building

Remember!
A **proper noun** begins with a **capital letter**.

People's names are proper nouns. **H**arry
The days of the week are proper nouns. **M**onday
The months of the year are proper nouns. **J**anuary

Names of shops and restaurants have **capital letters**.

 **G**reen **P**ark **R**estaurant

Some titles in books have capital letters.

 **P**arty **P**otato **N**ests

1 Write these restaurant names correctly. Use capital letters.

1 the pizza place _____
2 marco's italian restaurant _____
3 chinese corner _____

2 Write these recipe titles correctly. Use capital letters.

1 beef and tomato soup _____
2 sausage and mash _____
3 ice cream pyramid _____

3 This is your restaurant. Give it a name.

 Write the name here.

Language building   proper nouns

Grammar

Do you remember Harry's birthday meal?

Harry and his family went to a restaurant **to have** a meal.

They had the meal **to celebrate** Harry's birthday.

1 Ask and answer.

> They went to the Green Park Restaurant. Why?   To have a meal.

1 They went to the Green Park Restaurant.
2 Harry's mum went to the supermarket.
3 She bought carrots, peas and onions.
4 She chose some lovely bananas.
5 Harry went to the sports club.
6 Harry's sister went to the library.

a To play basketball.
b To make banana splits.
c To buy fruit and vegetables.
d To borrow some books.
e To make vegetable soup.
f To have a meal.

2 Read and make sentences. Write in your copy book.

Harry's mum went to the supermarket.
<u>Harry's mum went to the supermarket to buy fruit and vegetables.</u>

1 She cut up the fruit.
2 She bought some chocolate.
3 Harry's dad went to the sports club.
4 Harry's grandparents went to Egypt.

3 Discuss. Write in your copy book.

1 Why do children go to school?
2 Why do people go to work?
3 Why do people go to the sports club?
4 Why do people go on holiday?

Turn to Fluency Book 4 Programme 4.

Grammar   infinitive of purpose

Spelling

The letters **ar** can come at the **beginning** of a word.

The letters **ar** can come in the **middle** of a word.

The letters **ar** can come at the **end** of a word.

artist

starter

calendar

1 Write *ar* at the beginning.

1  — — my   2 — — ch

Read each word. Discuss what it means.

2 Write *ar* in the middle.

1 b — — k   2  p — — ty

Read each word. Discuss what it means.

3 Write *ar* at the end.

1  j — —   2  c — —

3 st — —   4 sc — —

5 vineg — —   6 coll — —

Read each word. Discuss what it means.

4 Write in your copy book. Use a word in a sentence of your own:

1 beginning with **ar**   2 with **ar** in the middle   3 with **ar** at the end.

Spelling   *ar* words

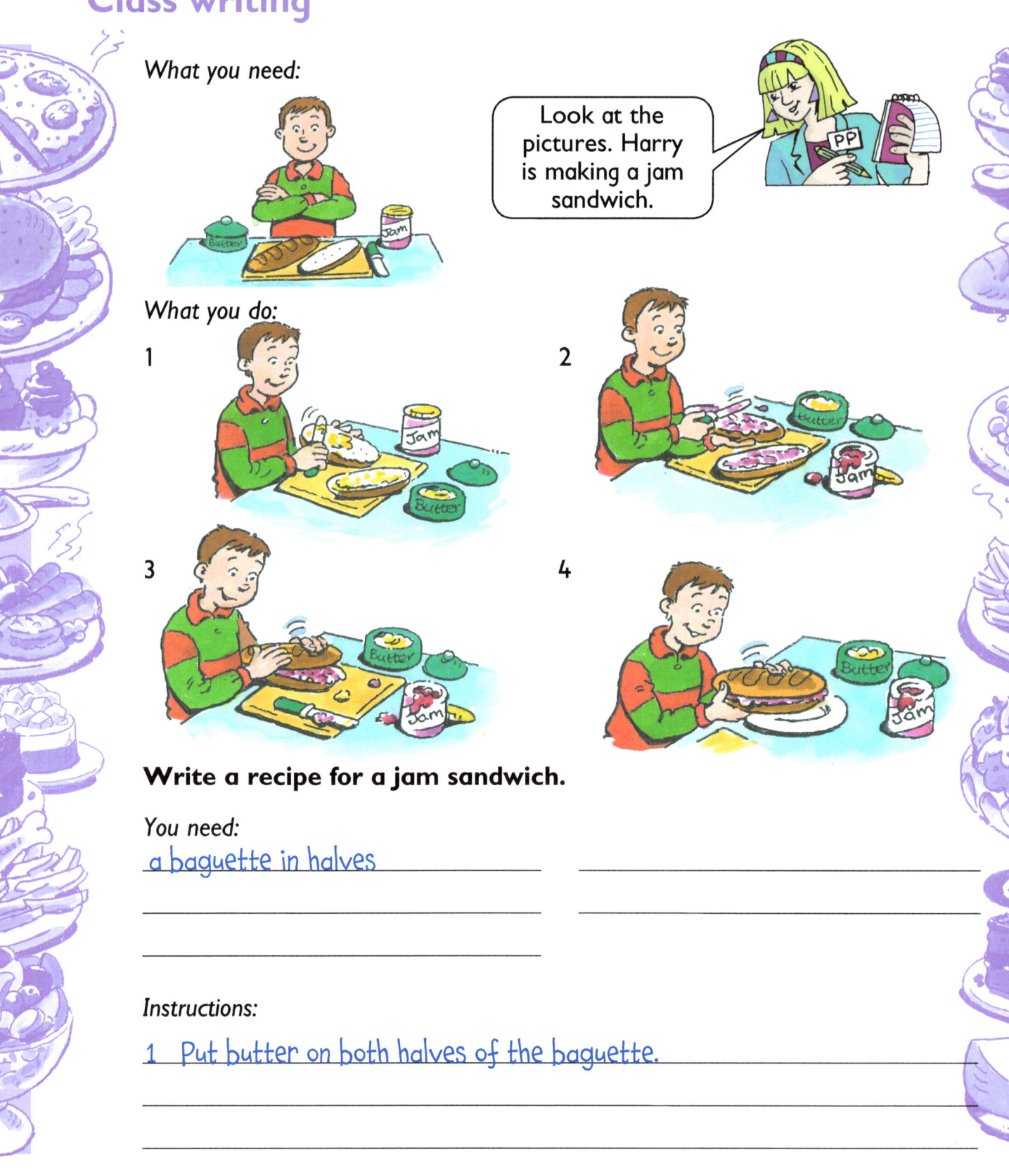

Reading for enrichment

Fascinating food facts

The longest carrot

Dr Bernard Lavery grew the longest carrot in 1987. It grew to 335 cm.

The largest bunch of bananas

In July 2001, people recorded the largest bunch of bananas. It had 473 bananas. It was growing in the Canary Islands.

The largest jelly

On 5th February 1981, Paul Squires and Geoff Ross made a huge, 35,000-litre, pink jelly. The flavour was watermelon. They made it in Australia.

The most ice cream eaten in 30 seconds

On 11th November 2002, Jamie Sargento de Silva from Portugal ate 67g of ice cream in 30 seconds. He used a teaspoon.

The largest curry

The largest curry weighed 3,106.5 kg. Abdul Salam made it on 17th July 2000. About 7,500 people ate the curry. Abdul Salam made the curry to raise money for charity. It raised £4,500 ($6,700).

Revision 1

1 Look at the pictures.
 1 What can you see?
 2 Do you sometimes go to town with your mum or your dad?
 3 What do you do there?

2 Listen and read.

3 Read and say.
Look at picture 1.
 1 Why did Tom and his mother go to town?
 2 How did they go to town?
 3 What was the weather like?
 4 What happened while they were driving to town?

Look at picture 2.
 1 Where was the bookshop?
 2 What did Tom want to buy?
 3 Did he buy the book? Why not?

Look at picture 3.
 1 Where did they go next?
 2 Did they find a football shirt?
 3 Did Tom buy it?

1 Harry's mother and Harry's brother, Tom, went to town. Tom wanted to buy a birthday present for Harry. It was raining so they took a taxi. While they were driving to town, the rain stopped and the sun came out.

Oh, good! The rain's stopping.

3 Next they went to a sports shop. Harry wanted a football shirt. They found a great shirt but it was very expensive.

This is nice.

It's very expensive. I can't buy it.

5 Tom and his mum started to walk home. Tom was sad. He did not have a present for Harry. Suddenly, they saw a very small shop on a corner.

Perhaps we can find something here.

They went inside.

2 They went to the mall. There was a big bookshop on the first floor. Harry wanted a book about volcanoes. They found the book but it was very expensive.

This is lovely.

It's very expensive. I can't buy it.

4 Next they went to a record shop. Harry wanted a CD by his favourite band, 'Wolf'. They looked and looked but they did not find it.

I can't see it.

They haven't got it.

6 They did not find a book about volcanoes. They did not find a football shirt. They found a CD by 'Wolf'. Tom was very happy.

This is a great present for Harry!

Look at picture 4.
1 Where did they go next?
2 Did they buy a CD?

Look at picture 5.
1 Was Tom happy or sad?
2 While they were going home, what did they see?

Look at picture 6.
1 What did Tom find in the corner shop?
2 Was he happy or sad?

4 Finish the sentences.
1 They went to the mall to …
2 They went to the bookshop to …
3 They went to the sports shop to …
4 They went to the record shop to …
5 While they were driving to town, …
6 While they were walking home, …

5 Listen. Where are they?

6 Act out the story.

Journey to Jo'burg

Naledi and Tiro lived with their granny. They lived 300 kilometres from the big city of Johannesburg. Their mother worked in Johannesburg. One day, their baby sister very sick. Their granny didn't have the mo for a doctor. The two children decided to walk to Johannesburg to find their mothe

The children walked quickly away from the village. The road was really just a track made by car tyres. Two lines of dusty red earth leading out across the flat dry grassland.

Once at the big tar road, they turned in the direction of the early morning sun, for that was the way to Johannesburg. The steel railway line glinted alongside the road.

'If only we had some money to buy tickets for the train. We don't even have one cent,' Tiro sighed.

'Never mind. We'll get there somehow!' Naledi was still confident as they set off eastwards.

The tar road burnt their feet.

'Let's walk at the side,' Tiro suggested.

The grass was dry and scratchy, but they were used to it. Now and again, a car or truck roared by, and then the road was quiet again and they were alone. Naledi began to sing the words of her favourite tune and Tiro was soon joining in.

On they walked.

Stimulus — modern fiction - extract

'Can't we stop and eat?' Tiro was beginning to feel sharp stabs of hunger. But Naledi wanted to go on until they reached the top of the long, low hill ahead.

Their legs slowed down as they began the walk uphill, their bodies feeling very heavy. At last they came to the top and flopped down to rest.

Hungrily they ate their sweet potatoes and drank the water. The air was hot and still. Some birds skimmed lightly across the sky as they gazed down at the long road ahead. It stretched into the distance, between fenced-off fields and dry grass, up to another far-off hill.

'Come on! We must get on,' Naledi insisted, pulling herself up quickly.

She could tell that Tiro was already tired, but they couldn't afford to stop for long. The sun had already passed its midday position and they didn't seem to have travelled very far.

On they walked, steadily, singing to break the silence.

The next day, a lorry driver was very kind to them.

The sun rose higher. On they walked. The heat sank into them and they felt the sweat on their bodies. On they walked. Alone again, except for the odd flashing by of a car or truck.

SCREECH! Tyres skidded and stopped.

'Where are you two kids going?'

The driver of the lorry stuck a friendly face out of the window.

'To Johannesburg, Rra.'

'Are you crazy? That's more than 250 kilometres away!'

'We have to go,' Naledi said simply, and explained.

'Well, well, that's something!' the driver muttered. 'It will take you a week to walk that far and your granny will be very worried. I should take you back home, but I'm late today already.'

He paused to think.

'Do you know where your mother works?'

Naledi nodded, pulling out the letter from her pocket.

'All right then. Hop on the back and I'll take you to Jo'burg. I'm taking the oranges there.'

'Thank you, Rra!'

The children laughed. They pulled themselves up onto the lorry, wedging themselves against the sacks of oranges. So they were really on their way! And it was their first time on a lorry too! It was very dangerous.

Beverley Naidoo

Comprehension

1 **Read together. Find a good word for each gap.**

1. Naledi and Tiro were going to look for their ___mother___ .
2. They had no _____ to buy train tickets.
3. Sometimes a car or _____ roared by them.
4. They ate sweet _____ and drank water.
5. Tiro was very _____ .
6. When the driver picked them up they were more than _____ kilometres from Johannesburg.
7. The lorry was carrying _____ .

2 **Discuss your answers to these questions.**

1. Why do you think the children sang as they walked along?
2. Why do you think the grass was dry and scratchy?
3. What sort of man do you think the lorry driver was?

Vocabulary

> **Adjectives** tell us more about **nouns**.

1 **Find two *adjectives* in the story that describe these nouns.**

1. earth ___dusty___ _____
2. hill _____ _____
3. air _____ _____

2 **Use the first letter of each word. Put them in *alphabetical order*.**

> village   railway   birds   words   potatoes

___birds___ _____ _____ _____ _____

3 **Use the *second* letter of each word. Put them in *alphabetical order*.**

> children   come   car   cent   crazy

___car___ _____ _____ _____ _____

Language building

Nouns can be **singular** or **plural**.
Verbs can also be **singular** or **plural**.

When we use a **singular noun**, we must use a **singular verb**.

My mother work**s** in Jo'burg.

singular noun   singular verb

When we use a **plural noun**, we must use a **plural verb**.

My parents work in Jo'burg.

plural noun   plural verb

1 Discuss which is the correct *verb*. Write it.

1 The children _walk_ a long way to school.   walk/walks
2 The child _____ a long way to school.   walk/walks
3 The truck _____ a lot of noise.   make/makes
4 The trucks _____ a lot of noise.   make/makes
5 The policeman _____ the strangers.   stop/stops
6 The policemen _____ the strangers.   stop/stops

2 Write the correct *noun*.

1 The _girl_ likes ice cream.   girl/girls
2 The _____ go very fast.   car/cars
3 The _____ taste really good.   orange/oranges
4 The _____ sing as they walk.   child/children
5 The _____ looks empty.   house/houses

Language building   noun-verb agreement

Grammar

Do you remember the lorry driver in *Journey to Jo'burg*?

'I **should** take you back home.'

'You **shouldn't** be walking alone.'

Remember!
shouldn't = should not

1 **What should they do? Match.**

1 They are very tired. _c_
2 They are hungry. ____
3 They are thirsty. ____
4 Big trucks roar past them. ____
5 It is a long way to Jo'burg. ____

a They should drink their water.
b They should not rest for long.
c They should sit down and rest.
d They should eat their sweet potatoes.
e They should be careful.

2 **Give advice. Use *should* or *shouldn't*.**

1 I'm very tired. — You should go to bed.

2 My hands are dirty.

3 Mum's got a headache.

4 My shoes are muddy.

5 My hair's in a mess.

6 My feet hurt.

brush	clean
wash	noise
shoes	

These words can help you.

Turn to Fluency Book 4 Programme 5.

Now write in your copy book.
Like this: She should ...
                He shouldn't ...

Spelling

The letters **dge** make a **j** sound.

The letters **dge** can come at the **end** of a word.

we**dge**

1 **Add *dge*. Read the words. Match words and meanings.**

1 __  bri_d_ _g_ _e_   a This keeps food cold.

2 __  he__ __ __   b It's used for moving on snow.

3 __ 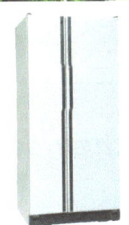 fri__ __ __   c This goes across a river.

4 __  sle__ __ __   d It's a long line of bushes.

2 **Use the *dge* words to complete the sentences.**

1 We will have to cut the _____ in the garden.
2 The _____ got stuck in the snow.
3 We keep cheese in the _____ .
4 The man was fishing from the _____ .

3 **Write a *dge* word that rhymes.**

1 fridge _____   2 edge _____

Class writing

Every story has **characters**.
Some characters are people. Some characters are animals.

The characters in the story on pages 42 and 43 are:
- Naledi – a girl, 13 years old
- Tiro – her brother; younger
- the lorry driver – takes oranges to Johannesburg.

1 What do you think they look like?
Write *adjectives* to describe them. Use your imagination.

Naledi	Tiro	the lorry driver
_____	_____	_____
_____	_____	_____
_____	_____	_____
_____	_____	_____
_____	_____	_____

2 We can tell what characters are like by what they say and do.

1 Do Naledi and Tiro love their baby sister? _____
   How do you know? _____
   _____
   _____

2 Who is stronger, Naledi or Tiro? _____
   How do you know? _____
   _____
   _____

3 Is the driver kind or unkind? _____
   How do you know? _____
   _____
   _____

Reading for enrichment

Soraya's blanket

Soraya felt mixed up. She was excited to think of a new country and glad to see that she would be with her cousins again. She hadn't seen them since their visit to Darwaza over a year ago. She was sad, too, because she knew she would be leaving her family and friends behind in the village. Tears filled her eyes as she hugged and kissed grandmother 'Goodbye'.

> Soraya lived in Darwaza, a village in India. Most of the time it was hot and sunny. When it was very hot she slept on the roof of her house. Soraya loved her grandmother very much. She spent a lot of time with her. One day the family moved to Britain. Grandmother stayed in India.

As Soraya's plane flew halfway round the world, she thought about her grandmother and wished that she could have come with them. Then, as the plane landed, Soraya's head filled with new sights and sounds, and there were her cousins waiting to show her round the new town. The sadness left her.

She began to go to school with her cousins and though it was hard at first to make sense of it all, Soraya knew that she would like it here. Oh, but it was so cold. As she shivered, she thought she would never get used to the cold British weather. It was only at night-time that Soraya felt lonely, when she looked at the sparkling frost patterns on the window pane in her bedroom. She dreamt about the warm nights sitting close to grandmother under the stars. Every night Soraya missed her grandmother and wished she were next to her, then she wouldn't be cold.

A few weeks after they arrived, Mum and Dad wrote to Grandmother to tell her about their new home. Soraya asked if she could write a sentence too. She wrote, 'I love and miss you, Naanee, especially at bedtime.'

Weeks passed. Then, one day the postman handed Soraya a parcel with her name on it. The postmark and stamps told her it was from India. She opened it as fast as she could. Inside, she found a beautiful woollen blanket knitted so finely in the brightest colours. As she wrapped it round herself, she found a note pinned to it that said, 'My Soraya, I have made this for you. Put it on your bed and think of me every night. In the blanket is my love for you. It will always keep you warm, Naanee.' Night times seemed to get warmer for Soraya from that day.

Reading extension — short story with life events

A long journey

Kim and her family make a long journey to the UK. They are staying there with their friends for a month. When they arrive, Kim writes to her friend, Katy.

12, Oasis Flats
High Street
Sandtown
25th July

Dear Katy,
    We arrived yesterday. It was a long journey but it was very exciting. I am writing to tell you about the journey.
    The plane left at 10.30 in the morning. We got up at 6.30. Mum made a list of things to pack. She crossed the things off the list when we put them in the suitcases. Amy packed too much. She couldn't close her suitcase.
    Dad walked around the house. He locked the windows and watered the plants. We were ready to go at 8 o'clock. The suitcases were in the hall and we waited for the taxi.
    The taxi was twenty minutes late. Mum and Dad thought we were going to miss the plane. We got the suitcases in the taxi and went to the airport. It was a good journey. We weren't late.
    There were a lot of people at the airport. Everyone was going on holiday. We checked in the suitcases first. Then we had something to eat and drink. We waited for two hours and then we got on the plane.

Stimulus   letter

I had the best seat. It was at the front, next to the window. Amy doesn't like sitting next to the window but I liked looking at the towns and the fields and the clouds. It was great! Everything looked very small. When we were above the clouds, they looked like snow. I watched a film but it wasn't very good. I read my book.

We were in the plane for five hours. I was happy to get off when we landed. Our friends met us at the airport. It was lovely to see them again.

I will write to you again and tell you about what we are doing.

Lots of love,
　　　Kim.

PS: This is my family at the airport. Look at Amy's suitcase!

Comprehension

1 Say *true*, *false*, or *I can't tell*.

1. Katy wrote a letter to Kim.
2. The family got up three hours before the plane left.
3. The family had coffee and cake at the airport.
4. Kim sat by the window on the plane.
5. Katy watched a Disney film on the plane.
6. Their friends were not at the airport when they landed.

2 Discuss your answers to these questions.

1. Why do you think Mum made 'a list'?
2. Why couldn't Amy close her suitcase?
3. What things do you think Kim saw and heard at the airport?
4. Why do you think Amy didn't want to sit by the window?

Vocabulary

1 Find a word in the letter that rhymes with each word.

1. fist   *list*
2. ball   _____
3. gate   _____
4. clowns _____

> Read the letter again carefully.

> Sometimes messages are in code. People write a number for each letter. 1 = A, 2 = B, and so on. Look!

A	B	C	D	E	F	G	H	I	J	K	L	M	N	O	P	Q	R	S	T	U	V	W	X	Y	Z
1	2	3	4	5	6	7	8	9	10	11	12	13	14	15	16	17	18	19	20	21	22	23	24	25	26

2 Can you read this secret message?

4 5 1 18   11 9 13 ,

9   8 15 16 5   25 15 21   1 18 5

8 1 22 9 14 7   1   7 15 15 4   20 9 13 5 .

12 15 20 19   15 6   12 15 22 5 ,

11 1 20 25

Language building

> **Remember!**
> When we **compare** two things we add **er** to the **adjective**.
>
>
>
> a small suitcase   a small**er** suitcase
>
> When we compare **more than two things**, we add **est** to the **adjective**.
>
>
>
> a small suitcase   a smaller suitcase   the small**est** suitcase
>
> Some adjectives do *not* follow the rules.
>
> | Adjective | Comparing two | Comparing more than two |
> |---|---|---|
> | good | better | best |
> | bad | worse | worst |
> | little | less | least |
> | many | more | most |

1 Write the correct form of the adjective.

1 It was a __better__ journey than the last one. good/better/best
2 That was the _____ holiday I ever had. bad/worse/worst
3 I have _____ luggage than you. little/less/least
4 The weather was _____ yesterday than today. bad/worse/worst
5 This plane holds _____ people than that one. many/more/most

2 Who has ...?

1 Sam has two apples. Kim has three apples. Ben has one apple.
   Who has the fewest apples?   _____
   Who has the most apples?   _____
2 Sam has four books. Kim has two books.
   Who has fewer books?   _____
   Who has more books?   _____

Grammar

Do you remember Kim? She wrote a letter to her friend, Katy.

I think I **will like** it here in England.

I'll write again soon.

We **will not stay** for more than a month.

I **won't enjoy** the long journey home.

Remember!
I'll = I will
I won't = I will not

1 **Circle *true*, *false* or *I can't tell*.**

1 Kim will spend her holiday in France.	true	false	I can't tell
2 She will stay there for two months.	true	false	I can't tell
3 She will go to the beach.	true	false	I can't tell
4 She will not visit London.	true	false	I can't tell
5 She will not do schoolwork.	true	false	I can't tell

Correct the false sentences.

2 **What do you think? Ask and answer about Kim's holiday.**

Will she like England?   Yes, she will.   or   No, she won't.

Will she
1 go to the beach?   2 study?   3 buy a present for Katy?
4 eat good food?   5 like England?   6 have a terrible time?

3 **Read and tick. What will you do tomorrow?**

Will you
1 come to school? ☐   2 stay at home? ☐
3 read a book? ☐   4 go shopping? ☐
5 watch TV? ☐   6 play with friends? ☐

Turn to Fluency Book 4 Programme 6.

Now write in your copy book.
Like this: Tomorrow, I will ...   I will not ...

Grammar   future (*will*)

Spelling

> A **soft g** sound saying **j** can be made like this:
>
> - **g** followed by **e**   lar**ge**
> - **g** followed by **i**   ma**gi**c
> - **g** followed by **y**   **gy**m

1 **Read. Underline the soft g.**

1. giant
2. vegetable
3. engine
4. giraffe
5. gemstone
6. orange
7. germ
8. message

Discuss what the words mean.

2 **Write.**

words beginning with soft g	words with soft g inside them
giant _____ _____	_____ _____
_____ _____	_____ _____

3 **Label the soft g and the hard g.**

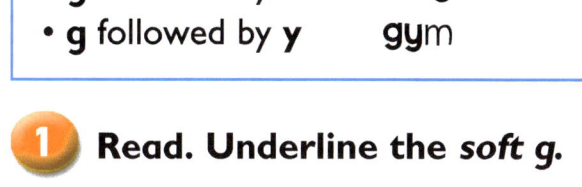

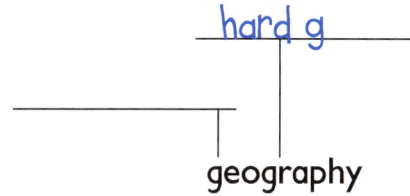
geography

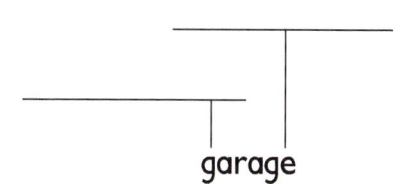
garage

4 **Solve the clues with soft g words.**

1. an animal with a very long neck   _____
2. a very tall person   _____
3. a school subject   _____

Spelling   soft g words

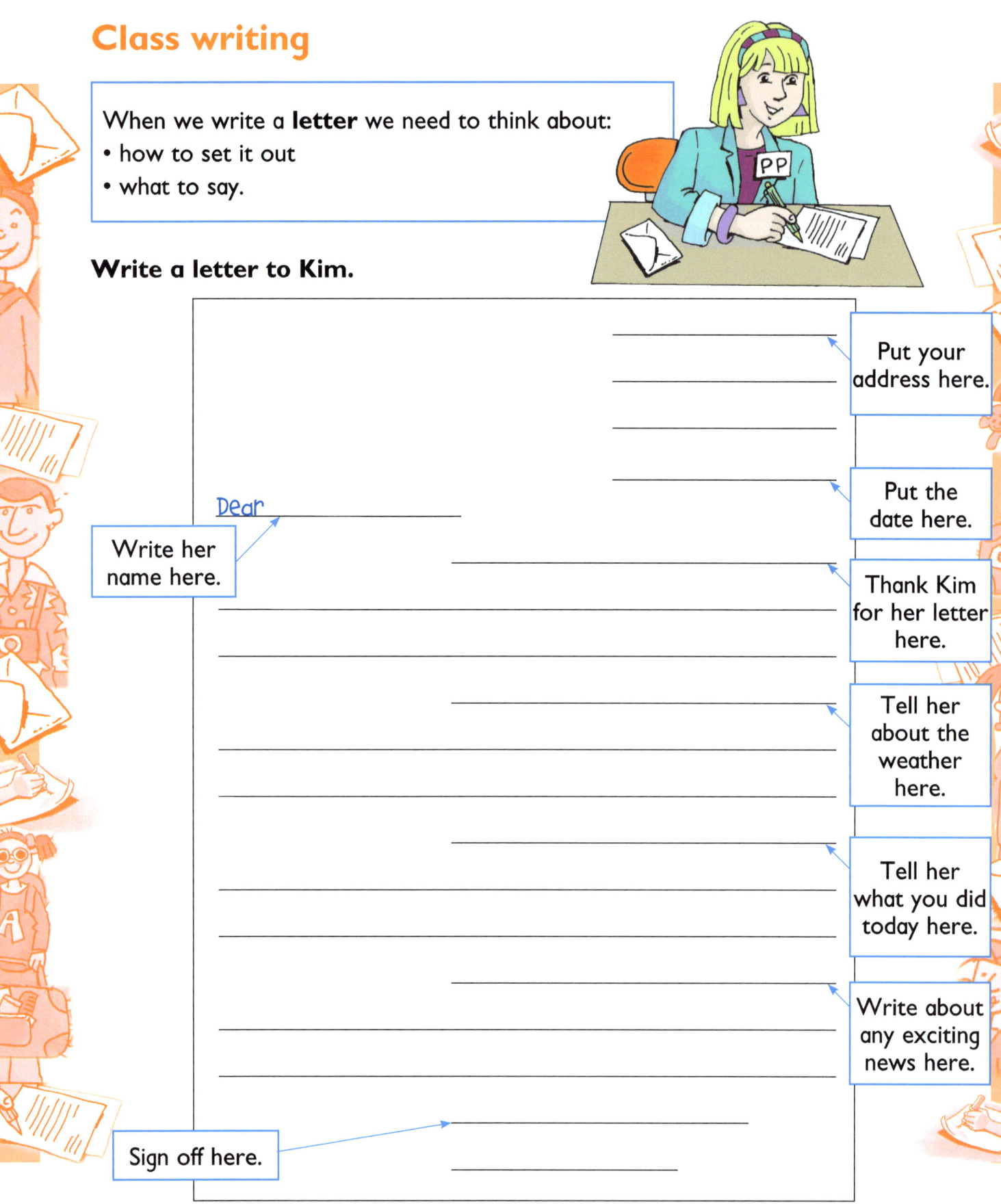

Reading for enrichment

How people learnt to fly

How do birds fly? Many years ago, people watched the birds and wondered how they flew. Today we can fly all over the world. This is how we learnt to fly.

1793: Two brothers flew in a hot-air balloon. They were the Montgolfier brothers.

1797: André Garnerin made the first parachute jump. He jumped from a hot-air balloon.

1852: Henri Giffard flew in an airship.

1903: The Wright brothers flew in a plane. They made four flights in one day. The last flight lasted 59 seconds.

1907: The first helicopter flew. It was built by Paul Cornu, a bicycle maker.

1909: Louis Bleriot flew across the English Channel.

1919: John Alcock and Arthur Brown flew across the Atlantic Ocean in 16 hours and 27 minutes.

1927: Charles Lindberg flew across the Atlantic Ocean on his own. He was the first person to do it.

1930: Amy Johnson flew from England to Australia on her own.

1932: Amelia Earhart flew across the Atlantic Ocean on her own. She was the first woman to do it.

1939: The first jet aeroplane flew.

1969: Astronauts flew in Apollo 11 and landed on the moon.

1970: The first jumbo jet flew.

Reading extension — historical information: facts about flying

The ant and the beetle

This story is about a beetle. He was a very lazy beetle. He did not like work. He liked to sit in the sunshine and have a good time.

One sunny day, the beetle went for a walk in a field. He found a shady place and sat down. He wanted to sleep in the sunshine. He closed his eyes. Then he heard a noise in the grass. The beetle jumped up and asked, 'Who's there?'

'I am,' said an ant.

'What are you doing?' asked the beetle.

'I'm getting grain,' said the ant.

'It's too hot to work,' said the beetle. 'Come and sit with me in the shade.'

'I can't stop working,' said the ant. 'Someone has to get food for the winter. We have to find lots of food in the summer. You know there is no food in the winter.'

'It's a long time until winter,' said the beetle. 'I'll think about winter when the weather gets cold.'

'It will be too late then. It's important to work hard now. It's wrong to sit in the sunshine,' said the ant. 'It's wrong not to work.' He hurried away.

The beetle liked the long, hot summer days. He did not work. He did not get food for the winter. The ant worked hard. He got lots of food.

Stimulus fable

Soon the weather was cold. The sky was full of clouds. The sun did not shine. The beetle went to look for food. He went from field to field but there was no food.

Soon it began to snow. The beetle was very cold and very hungry. He had no food. 'I am going to die,' he thought. The ant came out of his nest. He saw the beetle.

'What are you doing?' asked the ant.

'I have no food,' said the beetle. 'I am looking for food.'

'You didn't work in the summer,' said the ant. 'Ants always work in the summer. Anybody who doesn't work in the summer is hungry in the winter.'

'I know,' sobbed the beetle. 'Please help me. I will work hard next summer.'

The ant helped the beetle. The beetle lived with the ant for the winter. The beetle ate some of the ant's food. He did not die. I hope he learnt his lesson!

Comprehension

1 **Look back. Find the correct answers. Circle them.**

1	The beetle	a worked hard.	b did not work.
2	The ant worked in the	a summer.	b winter.
3	The ant was	a looking for food.	b sitting in the sunshine.
4	The beetle	a helped the ant.	b said it was too hot to work.
5	The beetle looked for food when	a it was hot.	b it was cold.
6	When the beetle looked for food	a he found some.	b he didn't find any.
7	In the winter it was	a hot.	b cold.
8	The ant	a helped the beetle.	b left the beetle to die.

(1 b is circled)

2 **Discuss your answers to these questions.**

1 Think of two words to describe the ant.
2 Think of two words to describe the beetle.
3 What did the ant mean when he said, 'It will be too late then'?
4 How is the weather described in the summer/winter?
5 Do you think the beetle learnt his lesson?

Vocabulary

1 **Find a word with the same meaning. Use the Thesaurus on page 167.**

Words with the **same**, or **nearly the same** meaning, are **synonyms**.

1 lazy _____   2 shady _____   3 cold _____
4 sunny _____   5 sobbed _____

2 **Make up some sentences.**
Use the *synonyms* you found in Activity 1 in sentences of your own.

Language building

> **Remember!**
>
> When we compare
> - **two things** we add **er** to the adjective
> - **more than two things** we add **est** to the adjective.
>
> hard   hard**er**   hard**est**
>
> If an adjective is a **long** word we use **more** and **most**.
>
> important   **more** important   the **most** important

1 Complete the table. Write the missing words.

adjective	comparing two	comparing more than two
lazy		the laz**iest**
	more beautiful	
frightening	**more** frightening	
		the **most** peaceful
cold		

2 Complete the sentences correctly.

1.

   This is an important letter.   This is a _more_ important letter.   This is the _____ important letter.

2.

   This is a frightening story.   This is a _____ story.   This is the _____ story.

3.

   This is a beautiful flower.   This is a _____ flower.   This is the _____ flower.

*Language building comparative/superlative with **more/most***

Grammar

Do you remember the ant and the beetle?

'**Someone** has to get food for the winter,' said the ant.

'Can **anybody** help me?' asked the beetle.

The beetle did not have **anything** to eat.

There was **nothing** to eat in the fields.

1 **True or false? Circle.**

1 In the summer, the insects did not have anything to eat.   true   false
2 In the winter, the ant had something to eat.   true   false
3 In the winter, the beetle had nothing to eat.   true   false

2 **Complete with something, anything or nothing.**

1 'There isn't _anything_ to eat in the fields,' said the beetle.
2 'I have got _____ to eat,' said the hungry beetle.
3 'Haven't you got _____ at all?' asked the ant.
4 'I've got _____ to eat,' said the ant. 'Here you are.'

3 **Complete these sentences.**

Remember!
somebody = someone
anybody = anyone
nobody = no one

1  Was there _anybody_ in the car?
   There was _____ in the car.

2  There was _____ behind the tree.

3  There was not _____ on the road.

Turn to Fluency Book 4 Programme 7.

62   *Grammar*   someone, anyone, no one (-body); something, anything, nothing

Spelling

Some words begin with **silent** letters.
We **cannot hear** silent letters in words when we say them.

'You **know** there is no food in the winter.'   We cannot hear the **k** in know.

'It's **wrong** to sit in the sunshine.'   We cannot hear the **w** in wrong.

1 Say these words. Discuss what they mean.

1 write	2 know	3 knife	4 wrong
5 wrap	6 kneel	7 wreck	8 knit

2 Write.

silent k words

know _____ _____ _____ _____

silent w words

_____ _____ _____ _____

3 Write the past tense.

1 I write   I _____   2 I know   I _____

4 Use these *silent letter* words in sentences.

1 wrong _____

_____

2 knit _____

_____

3 know _____

_____

4 wrap _____

_____

Spelling focus   silent **k** and **w** words

Class writing

A story has a **beginning**, a **middle** and an **end**.

The ant and the beetle

Beginning: It is summer.
The beetle sits in the sunshine.
The ant works hard.

Middle: The weather gets cold.
The ant has lots of food.
The beetle has no food.

End: It begins to snow.
The beetle is cold and hungry.
The ant lets the beetle live with him.

Look. Write a short story. *How the rabbit got long ears*

Beginning:

Middle:

End:

Reading for enrichment

All about ants

Have you seen ants near your house?
You can see them in the grass and near paths and steps. Look carefully – they are very small.

feelers
jaw

On a hot day, you can see little black ants in the garden.
These are garden ants. Garden ants are very small but they are very strong. Look at their big jaws and long feelers.

These are wood ants. They are running up and down a plant. Ants visit flowers to drink. They like the sweet drink in the flowers.
Sometimes an ant can get a drink from a greenfly. The greenfly makes a sweet drink. It is honeydew. The ant likes to drink the honeydew.

The queen ant lives in one room. She is the biggest ant in the nest. She stays in her room all the time. She lays many eggs.
Some rooms in the nest are full of the queen's eggs. In other rooms, new ants come out of the eggs.

The busy ants are worker ants. They bring food to the nest. They feed new ants. They make more rooms. They keep the nest clean.
Some worker ants can smell danger. Sometimes ants from other nests try to take their food. The worker ants fight them. They send the other ants away.

An animal dictionary

ant   a small insect with a sting. Many ants live under the ground in big groups called colonies.
bear   a big wild mammal with thick fur and a short tail.
cheetah   a big African wild cat that can run very fast.
dog   an animal kept for guarding buildings, working on farms, or for hunting.
elephant   a very large wild mammal with thick grey skin and a long nose called a trunk.
fox   a wild animal like a small dog with red-brown fur and a thick tail.
giraffe   a tall African mammal with a very long neck and very long legs.
hawk   a large bird that kills small animals for food.
ibis   a large bird with a long neck, long legs and a curved beak. It lives near water in hot countries.
jackal   a wild African or Asian mammal like a dog.
kangaroo   a big Australian mammal that moves by jumping. It carries its baby in a pouch.
lamb   a baby sheep.
moose   a big deer that lives in North America, northern Europe and Asia.
newt   a small amphibian with a long tail. It lives mainly in water.
orang-utan   an ape with long, orange hair.
python   a reptile; a snake that kills animals by wrapping itself around them.

> Words in dictionaries are in alphabetical order. You can use a dictionary to check the spelling of a word or to find out what a word means.

queen bee   a large female insect. The queen bee lays eggs for the colony.
rabbit   a small furry mammal with long ears, large teeth and a short tail.
squirrel   a grey or red-brown mammal with a long thick tail. It lives in trees.
tiger   a big Asian wild cat that has yellow and black fur.
unicorn   an imaginary animal like a horse with a single long horn on its head.
vole   a small mammal like a mouse but with a short tail.
walrus   a large sea mammal with two very long tusks.
x-ray fish   a fish with see-through skin so all its bones show.
yak   a big mammal like an ox with long hair and horns. It comes from Tibet and central Asia.
zebra   an African mammal like a horse with black and white stripes on its body.

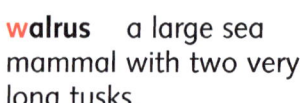

An animal encyclopaedia

Giant panda

> An encyclopaedia is an information book. The information is in alphabetical order. You can use an encyclopaedia to find information.

The giant panda looks like a bear. It has got black and white fur. It can grow up to 1.6 metres long and it weighs 75 to 100 kilograms.

The giant panda lives in cold bamboo forests in China. It eats bamboo shoots.

Giant pandas are in danger. They are very rare. There are fewer than 180 pandas in captivity and fewer than 1,600 pandas in the wild. Zoos are trying to help Giant pandas to have babies but it is very difficult.

Giraffe

A giraffe is a hoofed animal. It has got long legs and a long neck. It is 3 metres tall from the shoulder to the ground. Its neck is 2.5 metres long.

A giraffe's skin is pale with a red-brown pattern. It has got small horns on its head.

Giraffes live in African grasslands. They eat leaves and can live for a long time without water. They usually sleep standing up. Giraffes live in small groups with a male giraffe as their leader.

Comprehension

1 **Look at the dictionary page. What is ...**

1. ... an animal like a dog? _jackal_
2. ... an ape with long, orange hair? _____
3. ... an animal kept for hunting? _____
4. ... a big African wild cat? _____
5. ... a large female insect? _____
6. ... an imaginary animal? _____
7. ... an animal like an ox? _____
8. ... a large bird with a long neck? _____

2 **Look at the encyclopaedia page. Discuss your answers.**

1. What does the giant panda eat?
2. It says that the giant panda is 'very rare'. What does this mean?
3. It says a giraffe is a 'hoofed animal'. What does this mean?
4. How tall is a giraffe?
5. What is unusual about how a giraffe sleeps?

Vocabulary

> Remember! Words in **dictionaries** are in **alphabetical order**.

1 **Put these animals in the correct place in the dictionary.**

1. camel — Would it go before or after the cheetah? _before_
2. snake — Would it go before or after the squirrel? _____
3. whale — Would it go before or after the walrus? _____
4. horse — Would it go before or after the hawk? _____
5. tortoise — Would it go before or after the tiger? _____

2 **Use the Dictionary on page 160. Write what these words mean.**

> mammal   amphibian   reptile

Language building

> **Possessive nouns** tell you who owns something.
> They have an apostrophe (') and an s at the end.
> The **'s** tells you who the owner is.
>
> a **giraffe's** skin   =   the skin belonging to the giraffe
>   The giraffe is the owner.
> giraffe's   =   the possessive noun
> the **panda's** fur   =   the fur belonging to the panda
>   The panda is the owner.
> panda's   =   the possessive noun

1 Underline the owner.

1 the <u>insect</u>'s sting
2 the bear's fur
3 the fox's tail
4 the elephant's trunk
5 the kangaroo's pouch
6 the ape's hair
7 the rabbit's ears
8 the unicorn's horn
9 the zebra's stripes
10 the bee's honey

2 The apostrophes are missing. Discuss where they should go.

1 A giraffes horns are covered with skin.
2 A voles tail is very short.
3 A squirrels tail is very thick.
4 A rabbits teeth are very large.
5 An elephants skin is grey.

Now write the sentences correctly.

1 _____
2 _____
3 _____
4 _____
5 _____

Language building   possessive nouns - singular

Grammar

What do you remember about giant pandas?

There are **few** giant pandas left in the world.

In China there are **fewer** giant pandas **than** there were fifty years ago.

Last year **the fewest** baby giant pandas were born.

1 **Look at the chart. Answer the questions.**

	Zoo A	Zoo B	Zoo C		Zoo A	Zoo B	Zoo C
panda	3	1	2	giraffe	6	10	4
zebra	15	10	17	elephant	3	2	4

1 Which zoo has fewer pandas, A or B? ____
2 Which zoo has the fewest giraffes? ____
3 Write a sentence in your copy book with:
   a 'fewer zebras than'   b 'the fewest elephants'.

2 **Look at the pictures. Answer the questions.**

A has got **little** food.   B has got **less** food **than** A.   C has got **the least** food.

1 Which cat has got less food, A or C? ____
2 Which cat has got the least milk? ____
3 Write two sentences in your copy book, with:
   a 'less milk than'   b 'the least milk'.

Turn to Fluency Book 4 Programme 8.

Grammar   comparatives : **few, fewer, the fewest; little, less, the least**

Spelling

Some words end with a **silent b**.
We **cannot hear** silent letters in words when we say them.

lamb

We cannot hear the **b**.

1 Say the *silent b* words. Write them.

1    2    3

___lamb___   _____   _____

4    5

_____   _____

2 Write the *silent b* words in alphabetical order.

___climb___   _____   _____   _____   _____

3 Complete the sentences with a *silent b* word.

1 I ___comb___ my hair before I go to school.
2 She cut her _____ opening the tin.
3 He didn't want to _____ the ladder.
4 There was a _____ in the field.
5 There was a _____ of cake on his shirt.

4 Sort the letters to make *silent b* words.

1 r m c u b   ___crumb___   2 b t m u h   _____
3 m a b l   _____   4 i b l c m   _____
5 b o m c   _____

Class writing

Use the Dictionary on page 160 to help you.

1 Match the animal names with their meanings.

animal name   *definition*

1 horse      a   a small furry mammal with a long tail.

2 cat   b   a big, strong animal used for riding.

3 bull   c   a creature with eight legs.

4 rat   d   an animal with soft fur and whiskers.

5 spider      e   a male cow.

1 _b_   2 ___   3 ___   4 ___   5 ___

2 Write a dictionary page. Put the animals in alphabetical order.

| horse | tortoise | camel | lion | starfish |

animal   *definition*

_____   _____

_____   _____

_____   _____

_____   _____

_____   _____

Writing   dictionaries – words and definitions

Reading for enrichment

Animal fun

Teaser

What kind of ants
tear down trees?
What kind of ants
roll in the mud
to take their ease?
What kind of ants
have four knees?
What kind of ants
flap their ears
in the breeze?
What kind of ants
spell their name
with two 'e's?
Sh! Don't tell.
It's a tease.

Tony Mitton

Can you solve this?

(Answer: Elephants)

Undersea tea

OLIVER THE OCTOPUS
UNDERNEATH THE SEA
SWIMMING VERY SLOWLY
LOOKING FOR HIS TEA
MAKES A LITTLE BUBBLE
GIVES A LITTLE GRIN
"HI THERE, FISHES!
COME ON IN…"

Tony Mitton

Lions

Near an ancient standing Baobab tree
 the lion sits with burning mane.
  He looks all around
   but makes no sound,
 in the heat of the African plain.

Behind, in the grey and cooling shade,
 the rest of the pride is lying.
  After the kill
   they have eaten their fill
and now sleep the safe sleep of the lion.

Tomorrow they will awaken refreshed,
 as a new day breaks over the plain,
  and they'll sleekly rise,
   with death in their eyes,
 to start the hunt over again.

Robin Mellor

> What do you know about lions? Where do they live? When do they hunt? Read this poem about the king of the jungle.

This lion is very unusual!

The 'Veggy' Lion

I'm a vegetarian Lion,
I've given up all meat,
I've given up all roaring
All I do is go tweet-tweet.

I never ever sink my claws
Into some animal's skin,
It only lets the blood run out
And lets the germs rush in.

I used to be ferocious,
I even tried to kill!
But the sight of all that blood
made me feel quite ill.

I once attacked an Elephant
I sprang straight at his head.
I woke up three days later
In a Jungle hospital bed.

Now I just eat carrots,
They're easier to kill,
'Cos when I pounce upon them,
They all remain quite still!

Spike Milligan

Comprehension

1 **Answer these questions in your copy book.**

Lions
1. Where is the lion sitting?
2. Where is the rest of the pride sitting?
3. What do the lions do 'after the kill'?
4. What will they do the next day?

The 'Veggy' Lion
5. What has the lion given up?
6. How does the lion feel when he sees blood?
7. What happened when the lion attacked the Elephant?
8. Why does the lion only eat carrots?

2 **Discuss your answers to these questions.**

Lions
1. Why do you think the lion's mane is 'burning'?
2. Why do you think the lions can sleep safely?

The 'Veggy' Lion
3. Do you think the lion was good at hunting or not?
4. What do you think other lions think of the 'Veggy' lion?

Vocabulary

Groups of things have special names. A group of lions is called a **pride**.

These group names are called **collective nouns**.

1 **Write the *collective noun*.**

1.
a pack of playing cards
pack

2.
a bunch of grapes
_____

3. a flock of birds
_____

4.
a herd of elephants
_____

Language building

Some sentences **tell** us something.
These sentences are called **statements**.
Statements **begin** with a **capital letter** and **end** with a **full stop**.

Some sentences ask us something.
These sentences are called **questions**.
Questions **begin** with a **capital letter** and **end** with a **question mark**.

The lion makes no sound.

Where is the lion?

1 Discuss which are statements and which are questions.

1 The lion sits near the tree
2 Where is the rest of the pride
3 When will the lions hunt again
4 I'm a vegetarian lion
5 What do you eat now

Add a full stop to the statements.
Add a question mark to the questions.

2 Use these words to write *questions*.
Remember the question marks.

1   is   What   doing   lion   the
_____

2   sleep   the   When   lions   do
_____

3   lions   do   live   Where   the
_____

Look for the word with the capital letter to begin the sentence.

Language building   statements and questions

77

Grammar

Do you remember the poem about lions?

Who wrote the poem?
What do you know about lions?
Where do lions live?
How do they catch their food?
Why do they have sharp teeth?
Which lion is the fiercest?
When did you last see a lion?

1 Find the correct answer.

1 Where do lions live? _c_
2 What do they eat? ___
3 Why do they have sharp claws? ___
4 How do they catch their food? ___
5 Which lion is the leader? ___

a To catch smaller animals.
b They hunt together.
c They live on the African plains.
d The oldest and strongest male lion.
e They eat meat.

2 Write questions for the answers. Use question words from the box.

> How much? How many?
> How long? Why? Where?

1 _Where did you_ _____ I saw a lion at the zoo.
2 _____ Its tail was a metre long.
3 _____ There are ten lions.
4 _____ They eat a lot of meat.
5 _____ To see the lions.

3 Ask and answer. Think of questions beginning with *What? Who? Which? How?*

Turn to Fluency Book 4 Programme 9.

78 *Grammar* question words

Spelling

We can break words into **small parts**. These are **syllables**.
If you say a word **slowly** you can hear how many syllables it has got.
Each syllable has got a **vowel sound**.

There are lots of **two-syllable words**.

   be / hind   behind

1 Say the words slowly.

1 burning	2 sleep	3 hunt	4 eaten	5 skin
6 carrots	7 claws	8 roaring	9 meat	10 never

Discuss which words have *one syllable*.
Discuss which words have *two syllables*.

2 Write the words in Exercise 1 next to the correct heading.

one syllable words: _sleep,_ _____

two syllable words: _____

The letter **y** can sometimes stand in place of a **vowel**.

   clou / dy
cloudy

3 Split each word into *two syllables*.

1 party: __par__   +   __ty__   =   __party__
2 hungry: _____ + _____ = _____
3 thirsty: _____ + _____ = _____
4 only: _____ + _____ = _____
5 windy: _____ + _____ = _____

Spelling syllables - one- and two-syllable words

Class writing

Many poems **rhyme** like this.

I'm a vegetarian Lion,	*first line*
I've given up all **meat**,	*second line*
I've given up all roaring	*third line*
All I do is go tweet-**tweet**.	*fourth line*

The *second* line rhymes with the *fourth* line.

1 Finish these poems.

1 Choose a word that rhymes with **day**.

> I am a tiny, little ant,
> I rush around all **day**.
> I work and work and work and work,
> I don't have time to _____ .

eat
drink
play
sing

2 Choose a word that rhymes with **ground**.

> I am a long and bendy snake,
> I crawl along the **ground**.
> No one hears me coming
> 'Cos I never make a _____ .

noise
sound
squeak

2 Think of words that rhyme to finish these poems.

1 I have a head with lots of hair.
   I have two hands and _____ .
   I like to eat my vegetables,
   But I never eat my _____ .

2 I am a tree with lots of leaves
   Shiny, long and _____ .
   I'm sure I am the tallest tree
   That you have ever _____ .

Reading for enrichment

Crocodile is trying to catch Fox to eat him, but Fox is too clever.

The last laugh

Crocodile: Ha! Here comes my breakfast! I have a plan. Fox won't escape today!

Storyteller: Crocodile made a pile of grass. He picked a pretty flower. He put the flower on the pile of grass and hid under it.

Storyteller: Fox was singing a little song.

Fox: Tilly, Tally, down the valley.
All a-quiver, flows the river.
Tilly Tally.

Storyteller: Fox was very happy. It was spring. Crocodile heard Fox. He did not breathe. He smiled.

Fox: What a pretty flower. I will pick it up and put it behind my ear.

Storyteller: Fox picked up the flower. Quick as a flash, Crocodile jumped out and caught Fox in his mouth.

Crocodile: Hic. Hic. My breakfast.

Storyteller: Fox was scared. He thought very quickly.

Fox: I'm not scared of you. You say hic, hic! I'm scared of ha, ha, ha!

Storyteller: Crocodile was angry. He opened his mouth and said …

Crocodile: Ha, ha, ha!

Storyteller: Quick as a flash, Fox escaped and jumped back onto the river bank.

Fox: Ha, ha, ha! Goodbye, Mr Crocodile! Enjoy your breakfast!

Storyteller: Crocodile was angry. Fox ran away laughing and singing his song. Crocodile sat in the river. So that is how Fox had the last laugh.

Reading extension — play/fable

Revision 2

1 **Look at the pictures.**
1 What can you see?
2 Do you have a zoo in your town?
3 Do you go there sometimes?
4 Which animals do you like?

2 **Listen and read.**

3 **Read and say.**

Look at picture 1.
1 Where are the children?
2 Where are they going?
3 Who is with them?

Look at picture 2.
1 What are they doing now?
2 What is the weather like?
3 Should they take their bags with them?

Look at picture 3.
1 How many giraffes are there?
2 Are there more or fewer zebras?

1 These children are going to the zoo. They are going by bus with their teacher, Mrs Smart.

3 There are lots of animals at the zoo.

2 Now they are at the zoo. They are getting off the bus.

3 Where is the polar bear?
4 Is there anything in the water?
5 What are the orang-utans doing?
6 Have they got lots of fruit or only a little?
7 Do you eat more or less fruit than the orang-utans?
8 What kind of snake is it?
9 What is in the tank on the right?

4 Make sentences.
1 What should the children do at the zoo? Think of three things.
2 What shouldn't the children do at the zoo? Think of three things.

5 Listen and say which animals.

6 A trip to the zoo. Make up a story and act it out.

Unit 10

Open Day

We like to celebrate special occasions. Each year, Summerfield School has a special day to celebrate the end of the school year.

Scene 1

Setting	Professor Inventalot's office
Characters	Narrator, Professor Inventalot, Secretary
Scenery	two desks and chairs
Props	letters

[Professor Inventalot, a famous inventor, is sitting in his office. His secretary is with him. They are opening letters and reading them.]

Narrator: Summerfield School is having an Open Day. They have sent invitations to parents. They sent a special invitation to Professor Inventalot.

Professor: *[Speaks sadly.]* Every day is just the same. Nothing exciting ever happens.

Secretary: This is interesting, Professor! *[Reads a bit more of the letter.]* It's an invitation to Summerfield School's Open Day.

Professor: Can I read the invitation? *[As he reads it, his smile gets bigger and bigger.]* What a nice letter! Mmm. They want me to have lunch and make a speech. Excellent! I don't have any other places to go to on that day. *[Jumps up and claps his hands.]* Return the reply slip on the invitation, please. Tell them that I am happy to come.

Secretary: Yes, Professor.

We are happy to invite you to Summerfield School for our

Open Day

on 10th March at 11 am.
Special guest: Professor Inventalot

Please use the reply slip below.

_____ will/will not come

Name: _____
Summerfield School Open Day at 11 am on 10th M

84 Stimulus 🎧 play

Scene 2

Setting	a school classroom
Characters	Narrator, Teacher, a class of children
Scenery	classroom furniture
Props	none

[The teacher is at the front of the class, talking to the children.]

Teacher: Did you take your invitations home to your parents?

Children: *[All together.]* Yes!

Teacher: Are they going to come to celebrate our Open Day with us?

Children: *[All together.]* Yes!

Teacher: I've got some news for you. On Open Day, I am going to cook the soup for our lunch, and our guest will be the famous inventor, Professor Inventalot.

Children: *[All together.]* Hooray! Wonderful!

Teacher: If you help me, we'll make a special soup together.

Children: *[All together.]* Yes, yes. We'll help. What soup can we make?

Teacher: Mmm. Let me think. *[Scratches head and thinks.]* I've got a good idea. If you bring in different vegetables, we'll make vegetable soup.

Narrator: All the children agree to bring in different vegetables. Everyone is very excited about the Open Day.

Comprehension

1 **Look back. Find the correct answers. Circle them.**

1. The name of the school was — a Summertown. (b) Summerfield.
2. The school invited the — a Professor. b secretary.
3. The school was celebrating — a Sports Day. b Open Day.
4. The school invited the Professor to — a stay for lunch. b see a play.
5. The children took invitations for — a the Professor. b their parents.
6. The children will help make a special — a picture. b soup.
7. The children agree to bring in — a vegetables. b fruit.

2 **Discuss your answers to these questions.**

1. How do we know the Professor is an important person?
2. How does the Professor feel when he gets the invitation?
3. Why does the teacher scratch her head?
4. How do you think the story will continue?

Vocabulary

1 **Match the words with mixed up letters with the words from the play.**

1. g e t s t i n   b   a narrator
2. c r y n e e s   ___   b setting
3. r p o p   ___   c character
4. r a t r o r a n ___   d scenery
5. f o r o s s p e r ___ e prop
6. h a t c r a c e r ___ f professor
7. s e t r a c e r y ___ g secretary

Now find the meaning of each word in the Dictionary (pages 160-166).

Language building

> Remember! **Singular** means **one**. **Plural** means **more than one**. Some plural nouns are **irregular**. There are **no rules** to help you to understand how to change the singular noun into a plural noun.
>
>  one **child** (singular)    two **children** (plural)

1 Match the singular and plural of each noun.

singular		plural	
1 one child	c	a	two women
2 one man	___	b	two mice
3 one woman	___	c	two children
4 one tooth	___	d	two geese
5 one foot	___	e	two deer
6 one mouse	___	f	two men
7 one sheep	___	g	two feet
8 one deer	___	h	two sheep
9 one goose	___	i	two teeth

2 Which plural nouns are spelt the same as the singular nouns?

3 Discuss how to change the underlined *singular noun* into the *plural*.

1. There was a <u>mouse</u> in the kitchen. → There were **some mice** in the kitchen.
2. My <u>tooth</u> aches.
3. The <u>man</u> was climbing the stairs.
4. I saw a <u>sheep</u> in the field.
5. A <u>child</u> was playing in the playground.
6. The <u>woman</u> was sitting on a bench in the park.
7. My <u>foot</u> was muddy.
8. A <u>deer</u> eats grass in the forest.

Take care! Sometimes you have to make other changes too!

Language building — irregular plurals

Grammar

If you **help** me,
we'll **make** a special soup together.

We'll **make** vegetable soup
if you **bring** different vegetables.

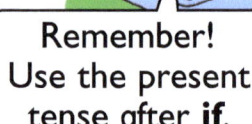

Do you remember? The teacher and her class are going to make something for lunch.

Remember! Use the present tense after **if**.

1 Correct the sentences. Change the underlined words.

1 If the school invites the Professor, he will be <u>sad</u> to go to the Open Day.
2 If the children bring vegetables, they will make <u>a chocolate cake</u>.
3 The children will make tomato soup if they bring <u>carrots</u>.
4 If they bring <u>potatoes</u>, they will make pea soup.
5 The Professor will enjoy his <u>breakfast</u> if the soup is good.

1 _happy_   2 _____   3 _____   4 _____   5 _____

2 Put the verbs in the correct tense.

1 (visit, have) If the Professor ___visits___ the school,

   he _____ a good time.

2 (bring, make) If the children _____ vegetables,

   they _____ soup.

3 (be, enjoy) The children _____ happy

   if the Professor _____ their soup.

3 Answer these questions. Then ask and answer with a friend.

1 If you go shopping at the weekend, what will you buy?
2 If you finish your homework early today, what will you do?
3 If you spend your next holiday at the beach, what will you do?

Turn to Fluency Book 4 Programme 10.

Grammar   first conditional: **if** + present; future (**will**)

Spelling

A **prefix** is a **group of letters** we can put at the **beginning** of a word.

 My glass is full.

 My glass is empty.

 Now I can **re**fill my glass.

(**re** + fill = refill)

 There are lots of words that begin with **re**.

1 Find two words that begin with *re* in the play on page 84. Discuss what they mean.

2 Make these words. Read the words you make.

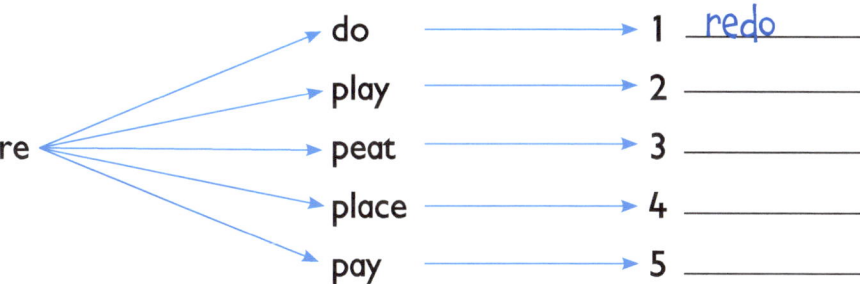

1 <u>redo</u>
2 _____
3 _____
4 _____
5 _____

3 Which word means:

1 to play again. _____
2 to say or do something again. _____
3 to pay back. _____
4 to do again. _____
5 to put something back in the same place. _____

4 Choose the correct word from above to complete each sentence.

1 I did not hear what you said. Can you _____ it, please?
2 When you borrow money, you must _____ it.
3 I did my work wrong. I will _____ it.
4 We stopped the match when it rained. We will _____ it tomorrow.
5 If I take a book off the shelf, I must _____ it.

Class writing

Write the next scene of the play together.
- In Scene 3, ten children bring different vegetables to school.
- They show the vegetables to their teacher.
- They tell the teacher what vegetables they have brought.
- The teacher is very pleased.
- They prepare the soup, but something goes wrong.
- Fortunately, they are able to resolve the problem.

Scene 3

1. **Fill in this box.**

   Look back at pages 84-85 and see how to do these things.

   Setting _____
   Characters _____
   Scenery _____
   Props _____

2. **Write the stage directions to the actors before they speak.**

   [_____
   _____]

3. **Here is the beginning of the scene. Continue the play.**

   Teacher: Have you remembered your vegetables?

   Children: [*All together.*] Yes!

   Teacher: Good. What vegetable have you brought, Sam?

   Sam:

Remember to write **stage directions** if you need them.

Reading for enrichment

Matiwara and the Old Woman

One day an old woman took a little girl from her parents. The little girl's name was Matiwara. The old woman took Matiwara to live with her in a little house in the forest. The old woman told Matiwara to clean the house and cook the food.

'How can I return to my village?' Matiwara asked. The old woman laughed and said nothing.

Matiwara asked the same question every day. One evening, the old woman was very happy. Matiwara asked the old woman, 'How can I return to my village?'

The old woman sang, '*Haa haa haa, hee hee hee, you must guess the name my mother gave to me.*'

Every day, Matiwara sat by the fire and guessed the old woman's name. The old woman laughed and said, 'You will not guess my name. It's a secret!'

One day, Matiwara went to get wood for the fire. She walked deeper and deeper into the forest. She saw a fire burning. She hid behind a tree. The old woman came. She danced around the fire and sang.

'*Haa haa haa, hee hee hee, Matiwara will never guess the name my mother gave to me. It's Sho-ko-lo-ko-ban-goshey.*'

Matiwara went back to the old woman's house. The old woman returned and asked Matiwara, 'Is my soup ready?'

Matiwara said, 'No. I was thinking of names. Is your name – Shoko, Shokoloko – Sho-ko-lo-ko-ban-goshey?'

Lightning flashed and thunder rumbled. The old woman looked surprised. 'Yes. That is my name,' she said. Lightning flashed again.

Matiwara closed her eyes. When she opened them she was in her village with her family. Everyone was happy to see her. They celebrated and had a big party.

Nobody saw the old woman again. But if you listen you can hear, '*Sho-ko-lo-ko-ban-goshey. Sho-ko-lo-ko-ban-goshey*' blowing through the tops of the trees in the forest.

Reading extension · traditional African story

Celebrating success – the story of Amy Johnson

Do you celebrate if you pass your exams at school? It's good when we do something clever, isn't it? This story tells you how Amy Johnson worked hard to learn how to be a pilot and fly a plane.

Her childhood
Amy was born in 1903. At school she liked to play rough games. When she was fourteen a football hit her in the mouth and hurt her lip. Some children laughed at her. They called her 'Ugly Amy'. She told her parents she hated school.

Amy decides to become a pilot
Amy didn't play with other children after they called her 'Ugly Amy'. She watched adventure films at the cinema. One day she saw a film about a pilot who did tricks in an aeroplane. She thought it was exciting and decided to be a pilot.

Amy learns to be a pilot
Amy went to university and then she worked in London, near an airfield. She liked to watch the small planes in the sky. Amy visited the airfield and asked to be a pilot. People laughed at her because there were no women pilots. She worked very hard and she passed her test. Amy was a pilot.

Amy learns about aeroplanes
Amy learnt about planes. She was an engineer for two years. She learnt how to build and mend engines. She worked hard and was always dirty, but she didn't stop.

Amy's challenge
Amy wanted to fly from England to Australia on her own. A man called Bert Hinkler did the journey in fifteen days. Nobody thought a woman could do the same journey.

The preparations

Amy bought a plane. She called it Jason. Amy put more fuel tanks on Jason. She planned the journey and bought the equipment. Her aeroplane had two open cockpits. Amy sat in the cockpit at the back of the plane. She put her tools, medicine, stove and mosquito net in the front cockpit. She asked people to let her land in different countries. At 8a.m. on 5th May 1930, she took off.

The flight

On the second day, she arrived in Istanbul, in Turkey. Amy felt sick. The petrol in the plane's engines smelt. On the fourth day, she landed in Baghdad in a sandstorm. Amy then flew to Karachi, in Pakistan. She stopped for three hours. On the seventh day, she flew into a rainstorm and crashed. She mended her plane and then flew on, but she got lost! She arrived in Singapore on the fourteenth day. On the twentieth day, Amy flew her aeroplane over a sea full of sharks, and landed in Darwin, Australia.

Celebrations

People sent her messages from all over the world. Everyone celebrated. The newspapers told stories of her adventures.

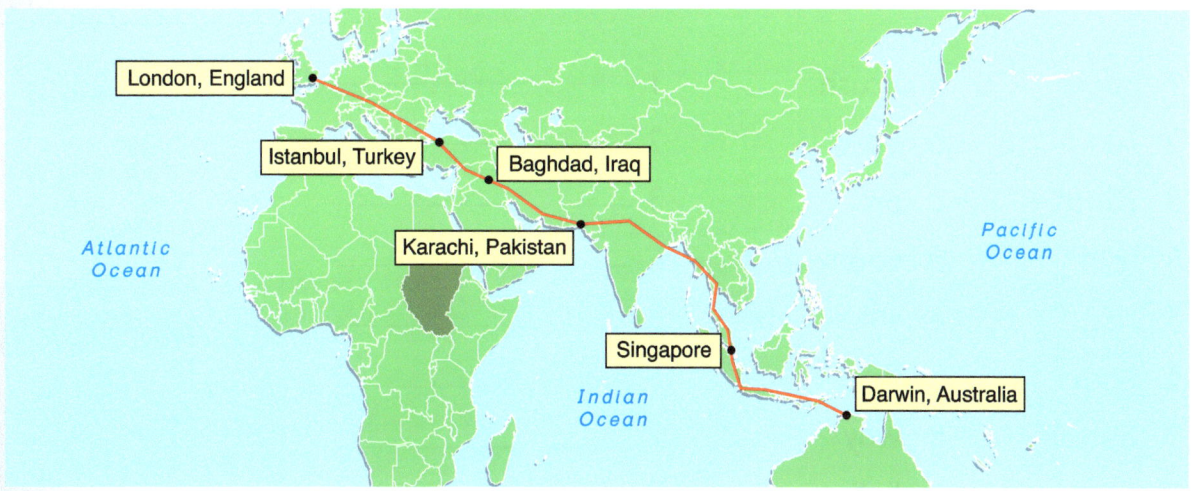

Comprehension

1 **Number the sentences in the correct order.**

___ Amy bought a plane.
___ Amy arrived in Australia on 24th May 1930.
_1_ Amy was born in 1903.
___ Amy worked in London, near an airfield.
___ Amy passed her test to fly planes.
___ Amy saw a film about a pilot who did tricks.
___ Amy took off for Australia on 5th May 1930.

2 **Discuss your answers to these questions.**

1 Why do you think Amy told her parents she hated school?
2 What do you think of children who make fun of other children?
3 Why do you think there were no women pilots at that time?
4 What do you think was Amy's most frightening experience?
5 How would you describe Amy? What sort of person was she?

Vocabulary

1 **Join the words. Write the *compound words*.**

> A compound word is made of **two words joined together**.
> air + field = airfield

1	cock	a	brush	1 _c_ _cockpit_
2	sun	b	bow	2 ___ ___
3	tooth	c	pit	3 ___ ___
4	foot	d	room	4 ___ ___
5	rain	e	shine	5 ___ ___
6	bath	f	fly	6 ___ ___
7	butter	g	way	7 ___ ___
8	run	h	ball	8 ___ ___

Language building

> **Adverbs** give more meaning to **verbs**.
> An **adverb of time** tells us **when** something happened.
>
> Amy **soon** visited the airfield.

1 **Discuss which word is an *adverb of time*. Underline it.**

1 Amy <u>always</u> wanted to be a pilot.
2 First, Amy went to university.
3 Then she worked near an airfield.
4 Amy soon visited the airfield.
5 Later, she passed her test and was a pilot.
6 Amy learned about engines next.
7 Afterwards, she bought a plane.
8 Then she prepared to fly to Australia.
9 Finally, she made the journey.

2 **Make up ten sentences. Use these *adverbs of time*.**

> today   now   tomorrow   next   never   again
> always   soon   yesterday   sometimes

3 **Describe:**

- how to make a cup of tea, *or*
- how you brush your teeth.

What **adverbs of time** did you use?

Language building   adverbs of time

Grammar

Amy Johnson was a successful pilot.
It **is** good to be successful, **isn't it?**

Amy loved flying planes.
Planes **are** exciting, **aren't they?**

You **are** interested in planes, **aren't you?**

1 **Circle the correct endings.**

1 He is a pilot, ...   isn't it? (isn't he?) aren't you?
2 Men and women are pilots, ...   aren't we? isn't he? aren't they?
3 It is a long flight, ...   isn't she? isn't it? aren't they?
4 We are learning about Amy Johnson, ...   aren't we? isn't she? isn't it?
5 She is a famous pilot, ...   isn't he? aren't they? isn't she?
6 You are looking at her photo, ...   isn't she? aren't they? aren't you?

2 **Add the correct ending to make a *question*. Say then write.**

1 Travelling by plane is exciting, _____
2 Planes are very fast, _____
3 You are fond of travelling, _____
4 Your uncle is a pilot, _____
5 We are learning about the first woman pilot, _____
6 Your aunt is learning to fly, _____

3 **Now ask and answer with a friend.**

Travelling by plane is exciting, isn't it?

Yes, it is.
or
No, it isn't.

Turn to Fluency Book 4 Programme 11.

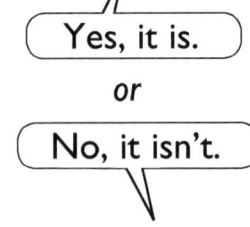

Spelling

When the letter **c** is followed by **e**, **i** or **y** it usually sounds like **s**. We call this a **soft c**.

 **c**inema

1 Read. Underline the *soft c* in each word.

_c_ity   dance   circle   sentence   bicycle

race   centre   nice   celebrate   cinema

2 Write the words which ...

... **begin** with a *soft c*   _city,_ _____

... have a *soft c* **inside** them   _____

3 Read the clues. Match each clue with the correct *soft c* word.

1. A large town. _f_
2. A round shape. ___
3. You do this to music. ___
4. The middle. ___
5. You can ride it. ___
6. To do something special to show you are happy. ___
7. A place where you can see films. ___
8. A group of words. ___
9. A running competition. ___
10. Pleasant. ___

a dance
b cinema
c celebrate
d nice
e circle
f city
g centre
h race
i bicycle
j sentence

Spelling focus   soft c

Class writing

*Here are some **notes** about the rest of Amy Johnson's life.*

1 Read the *notes* together. Discuss what they mean.

The years 1931-1938
- 1931 – flew from England to Japan and back
- 1932 – flew from England to South Africa and back
- both flights – fastest time ever – broke records
- 1933-1938 – many more flights – broke many more records

The Second World War
- the Second World War began 1939
- joined the Royal Air Force
- flew aeroplanes for Britain
- 1941 – crashed near London – died

Amy's achievements
- the first woman pilot
- showed people that a woman was able to fly
- very brave
- broke many records
- made people interested in planes

*Look back at pages 92 and 93. The information is in **paragraphs**. Each paragraph has got its own **heading** (or title).*

2 Write three *paragraphs* about Amy in your copy book. Use the notes. Write in sentences.

Here is the beginning of the first paragraph:

<u>**The years 1931-1938**</u>
<u>In 1931, Amy flew from England to Japan and back. The next year, in 1932, she made another long journey. She flew from England to South Africa and back.</u>

Writing a biography (using notes)

Reading for enrichment

Celebrating the sunshine!

Thank you letter

Dear Sun,
Just a line to say:
Thanks for this
And every day.
Your dawns and sunsets
Are just great –
Bang on time,
Never late.
On dismal days,
As grey as slate,
Behind a cloud
You calmly wait,
Till out you sail
With cheerful grace
To put a smile
On the whole world's face.
Thanks for those
Blazing days on beaches.
For ripening apples,
Pears and peaches;
For sharing out
Your noble glow;
For sunsets – the
Loveliest things I know.
Please carry on:
We know your worth.

Love from
A Friend on Planet Earth.
   Eric Finney

> On sunny days, it is good to be alive.
> This poem is a thank-you letter to the sun.

The flying house

Hurricanes are violent storms with very strong winds. Sometimes hurricanes are called cyclones. Hurricanes can cause enormous destruction. If buildings are not strong enough, a hurricane will smash them to pieces. Hurricanes are usually too powerful for everything in their path. In *The Wizard of Oz*, Dorothy's house was picked up by a cyclone! The cyclone carried the house along for miles! Read the story.

They heard the wind wailing. It was coming from the north. Uncle Henry and Dorothy looked up and saw the wind coming. The strong wind was blowing the long corn in the fields. The corn looked like waves at sea. Then they heard the wind whistling from the south. They looked that way and saw the strong wind blowing the long corn from the south, too.

Suddenly Uncle Henry stood up.

'There's a cyclone coming, Em,' he shouted to his wife. 'I'll go and look after the horses and cows.' Then he ran towards the sheds where the horses and cows were kept.

Aunt Em stopped what she was doing. She came to the door. The cyclone was coming closer and closer. It was coming towards the house!

'Quick, Dorothy,' she screamed, 'run to the cellar!'

Toto, the dog, was scared. He jumped out of Dorothy's arms and hid under the bed. Dorothy bent down and tried to get him. Aunt Em was very frightened. She quickly opened the door in the floor and climbed down the ladder into the dark cellar under the house. At last Dorothy caught Toto, and picked him up. She followed her aunt, but the wind shrieked loudly and shook the house hard. Dorothy fell over and sat down on the floor.

Then something strange happened.

The wind spun the house round two or three times, and then slowly lifted it up into the sky like a balloon. The house was in the centre of the cyclone. In the middle of a cyclone, the winds are often calm, but not in this cyclone! The winds lifted the house higher and higher. The house was at the top of the cyclone! The cyclone carried the house along with it for miles and miles, just like a feather!

It was very dark, and the wind howled around her, but Dorothy was quite comfortable. The house rocked gently on top of the cyclone. Dorothy felt like a baby in a cradle.

Comprehension

1 **Say *true*, *false* or *I can't tell*.**

1. A cyclone is the same as a hurricane.
2. Dorothy's uncle was called Harry.
3. The strong winds came from the west.
4. Toto was Dorothy's dog.
5. Aunt Em and Uncle Henry went into the cellar.
6. The winds lifted the house to the top of the cyclone.
7. The house travelled a hundred kilometres on the cyclone.

2 **Discuss your answers to these questions.**

1. Why are hurricanes (or cyclones) frightening?
2. What signs were there that a cyclone was coming?
3. Why do you think Aunt Em went down into the cellar?
4. What do you think happened to Uncle Henry?
5. How do you think Dorothy felt when the winds lifted up the house?

Vocabulary

1 **Use the Thesaurus on page 167. Find a word with the same meaning.**

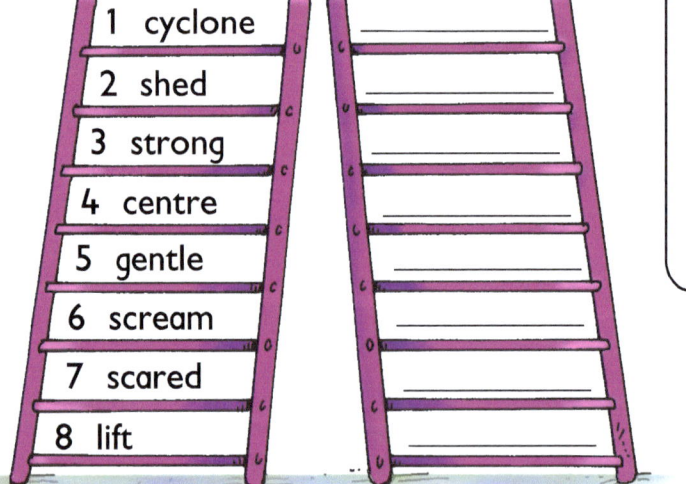

1. cyclone
2. shed
3. strong
4. centre
5. gentle
6. scream
7. scared
8. lift

A **thesaurus** gives you words with the **same meaning**. Remember! Words with **similar meanings** are called **synonyms**.

2 **Make up some sentences.**
Use the *synonyms* you found in Activity 1 in sentences of your own.

Language building

> **Direct speech** is when we write down the **exact words** someone said.
> We use **speech marks** to show the **beginning** and **end** of what was said.
>
>   'Quick, Dorothy, run to the cellar!' Aunt Em screamed.
>
> Sometimes we can write this another way. We sometimes split a sentence in direct speech into **two parts**, like this:
>
>   'Quick, Dorothy,' Aunt Em screamed, 'run to the cellar!'
>
> Notice that all the words Aunt Em said are still in speech marks.

1   The *direct speech* is split into *two parts*. Change it into *one part*.

1. 'Listen, Dorothy,' said Uncle Henry, 'there's a cyclone coming.'
   '<u>Listen, Dorothy, there's a cyclone coming,</u>' said Uncle Henry.

2. 'Come here, Toto,' Dorothy said, 'and don't hide under the bed.'
   '_____,' Dorothy said.

3. 'Sit down,' the teacher said, 'and get on with your work.'
   '_____,' the teacher said.

4. 'I like Sam,' Emma said, 'but Amy is my best friend.'
   Emma said, '_____.'

5. 'Open the door, Tom,' Mum said, 'and see who is there.'
   Mum said, '_____.'

2   Discuss how to split the *direct speech* into *two parts*.

1. 'I've finished my homework so can I watch TV now?' Amy said.
2. 'Are we lost or is this the right way to the shops?' Carla asked.
3. 'Quick, Tom, your house is on fire!' Mr Smith shouted.
4. 'I'm hungry and I want something to eat,' Jenny said.
5. 'When I went to town I bought some new shoes,' Mrs Peters said.
6. The dentist said 'Open your mouth and let me see your teeth.'

Language building   direct speech (split sentences)

Grammar

Do you remember the hurricane in 'The flying house'?

Hurricanes are usually **too** strong for everything in their path.

If buildings are not strong **enough**, a hurricane will smash them to pieces.

1 Read, then ask and answer. The answers are in the box.

1. Dorothy did not climb down into the cellar. Why not?
2. Aunt Em did not wait for Dorothy. Why not?
3. Toto was under the bed. He did not want to come out. Why not?
4. The house did not stay on the ground. Why not?
5. Dorothy could not hear anything. Why not?

> a Because he was too scared.
> b Because the wind was too loud.
> c Because she was not quick enough.
> d Because she was too frightened.
> e Because it was not strong enough.

2 Say then write. Put *too* or *enough* in the sentences.

1. I can't lift this suitcase. It is heavy. ___It is too heavy.___
2. John won't win the race. He isn't fast. _____
3. I can't eat these grapes. They aren't sweet. _____
4. Anna can't go to school. She is ill. _____

3 Make two sentences for each picture. Use *too* and *enough*.

1    2    3

He can't wear that hat.   She can't reach the shelf.   They can't go to school.

Turn to Fluency Book 4 Programme 12.

Grammar *too* + adjective; adjective + *enough*

Spelling

> Some words contain **silent letters**.
> We **cannot hear** silent letters in words when we say them.
>
> In the centre of a hurricane it is of**t**en ca**l**m.
>
> We cannot hear the **t** in **often** or the **l** in **calm** when we say the words.

1 Say the words. Discuss what each word means.

calm   often   palm   wrestle   half

talk   castle   walk   listen   whistle

2 Write the words with a *silent l*. Underline the *silent l*.

  ca<u>l</u>m   _____   _____   _____   _____

3 Write the words with a *silent t*. Underline the *silent t*.

  _____   _____   _____   _____

4 Write the word with a *silent w* and a *silent t*. _____

5 Discuss. Choose a *silent l* or *silent t* word for each sentence.

1 I can hold things in the ... of my hand.
2 '...' rhymes with 'walk'.
3 I use my legs to ... .
4 It was not windy – it was ... .
5 I cut my apple in ... .
6 I use my ears to ... .
7 To ... means to fight.
8 A ... is a big building with thick stone walls.
9 I blow a ... and make a noise
10 I ... laugh a lot.

Write the sentences in your copy books.

Class writing

> Every story has a **setting**. This is where the story **takes place**.

1 **Discuss. Look back at the passage on pages 100 and 101. It is from the *beginning* of a story.**

1 How do you know Dorothy did not live in a town?
2 How do you know Dorothy lived on a farm in the countryside?

2 **What was Dorothy's house like?**

- Was it small? big? huge?
- Was it made of bricks? wood? something different?
- What colour was it? What colour was the front door?
- Did the house have a roof? What was it made of?
- Did it have a room in the roof?
- How many bedrooms did the house have?
- Where was Dorothy's bedroom?
- Did the house have a cellar? Where? What was it like?

3 **What was the farm like?**

- Was there anything near the house, outside?
- What farm vehicles were there?
- What did the farm grow?
- Were there any farm buildings?
- What animals were there? Where were they?
- What noises did they make?
- Was the farm smelly?

4 **Now write a *description* of the story *setting* together.**

> When you have finished, read it again. Can you improve it? Can you put in any better adjectives?

106 Writing descriptive writing (describing a setting)

 **Reading for enrichment**

The weather forecast

> These symbols were designed for BBC television weather forecasts.

	Symbol	Meaning
1	15 / -2	**Temperature** a Red numbers on a yellow background show temperatures above freezing. b Black numbers on a light blue background show temperatures below freezing.
2	☀ 25	**Sunshine** This yellow symbol means sunshine. The red number shows the temperature.
3	☁ ☁	**Cloud** a A white cloud means thin and patchy clouds. b A black cloud means thick clouds and dull weather.
4	☁☀	**Sunny intervals** The sun and cloud symbols together mean a mixture of sunshine and cloud.
5	☁💧	**Rain** The dark blue drops beneath the black cloud mean rain.
6	☁💧☀	**Showers and sunny intervals** The cloud, sun and rain symbols together mean some showers and some sunshine.
7	☁❄	**Snow** White flakes beneath the black cloud show snow.
8	☁❄💧	**Sleet** The cloud, snow and rain symbols together mean sleet.
9	☁⚡	**Thunderstorm** A black cloud with a yellow flash shows that there might be thunder and lightning.
10	30 →	**Wind** The black arrow shows wind direction. The white number shows the speed of the wind.
11	**FOG**	**Fog** The word FOG is written on the map where fog is expected.

Reading extension   chart: weather symbols and their meanings

Hurricane Harry - a newspaper report

SUPER STORM STRIKES!

Mr Brown's home with its roof missing

People knew Hurricane Harry was coming. They put boards on their windows and put everything away.

Yesterday Hurricane Harry struck the island. It was very violent. The storm arrived at 4 o'clock in the morning when most people were asleep. Howling winds and rain hit the coastline first and then travelled inland towards the town. The hurricane damaged houses and buildings all over the island.

Mr Brown was asleep with his family when the hurricane hit his house. The wind ripped the roof off his house and blew it onto his new car.

Mr Brown said, 'I was sleeping in bed and I heard a loud noise. I looked up and saw that my roof was missing!'

The hurricane blew the roof and Mr Brown's car to the beach. The Brown family left their home and went to the school to sleep. Mr Brown said, 'It was very uncomfortable in the school gym!' He also said that his family was pleased to sleep in a building with a roof.

The strong wind caused large waves in the sea. Many boats sank. The wind blew some boats, including Mr Brown's fishing boat, onto the beach. The gigantic waves smashed his boat and threw it onto the road. Mr Brown's neighbour, Mrs Downing, said her husband tried to save his boat but the wind picked it up and smashed it on the rocks. The main road is now closed.

'Have you ever seen such devastation?' Mrs Downing asked our reporter.

Stimulus   newspaper report

Mike King and his lorry

Trees blew down and smashed many cars. Mike King, a lorry driver, was lucky. The hurricane blew a tree onto his lorry.

'When the winds started, I tried to drive my lorry to a garage. Suddenly the hurricane blew down a mango tree which crashed onto the back of my lorry. It nearly hit my head. I won't forget Hurricane Harry! I'm very glad I'm not a sailor!' he said.

Many people were injured during the storm. They went to the hospital. The doctors and nurses were busy all night.

Dr Lee said, 'It was a terrible night. Many doctors and nurses worked through the night. We didn't stop for a moment. I don't want another night like that!'

Clearing up the island will not be easy. The police are giving plastic sheets to people who have lost their roofs. The electricity and water companies are trying to make the electricity work and keep the water clean. Schools are closed.

One person was happy with the hurricane. Ten-year-old Samantha Simmons said, 'There is one good thing about the hurricane - our school is closed and we have an extra holiday!'

by our reporter Carla Hill

Comprehension

1 **Read this together. Think of a good word for each gap.**

Hurricane Harry arrived at four o'clock yesterday (1) _morning_ . The wind blew the (2)_____ off Mr Brown's house. Mr Brown's family spent the night in the (3)_____ . The gigantic waves smashed Mr Brown's (4)_____ and threw it onto the (5)_____ . The winds blew a tree onto Mr King's (6)_____ . Many (7)_____ were injured during the storm. The doctors and nurses worked through the (8)_____ at the hospital.

2 **Discuss your answers to these questions.**

1. What did Mrs Downing mean when she said, 'Have you ever seen such devastation?'
2. Why won't Mike King forget Hurricane Harry?
3. How do you think people were injured in the hurricane?
4. Why will clearing up the island take some time?

Vocabulary

Sometimes we can group words of the **same subject** together. For example: teacher, school, student.

1 **Discuss the meaning. Circle any words to do with a hurricane.**

> morning   (cyclone)   island   beach   storm
> devastation   damage   school   winds   lorry   gale
> boat   roof   rain   waves   doctor   nurse

2 **Write as many different words about the weather as you can.**

Here are some words to help you begin.

sunshine   windy   freezing

Language building

We can write **speech** in **two** ways:

1 as **direct speech**.

Mike said, 'A tree fell on my lorry.'

This is written in **direct** speech.
Mike's **exact** words are used.
Speech marks are used.

2 as **reported speech**.

Mike said that a tree fell on his lorry.

This is written in **reported** speech.
Mike's exact words are **not** used.
No speech marks are used.

1 Discuss what differences you can see in each pair of sentences.

> The **first** sentence in each pair is in **direct speech**.
> The **second** sentence is in **reported speech**.

1 Mr Brown said, 'The wind blew the roof off my house.'
   Mr Brown said that the wind blew the roof off his house.

2 Mrs Brown said, 'My bed is uncomfortable.'
   Mrs Brown said that her bed is uncomfortable.

3 Mike King said, 'I am glad I'm not a sailor.'
   Mike King said that he is glad he is not a sailor.

4 Dr Lee said, 'Many people were injured during the storm.'
   Dr Lee said that many people were injured during the storm.

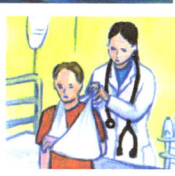

2 Discuss if each sentence has direct speech (D) or reported speech (R).

1 'I want a drink,' Edward said. __D__

2 Paul said that there was a bad storm last night. ____

3 Dr Lee asked Emma if her foot hurt. ____

4 'The large waves sank my boat,' Mr West said. ____

5 The TV reporter said that the hurricane did a lot of damage. ____

6 'Have you seen my car?' Mrs Scott asked. ____

Grammar

Do you remember Hurricane Harry?

Look at my house!
The wind **has blown** the roof off.

Look at my boat!
The waves **have smashed** it to pieces.

Have you ever **seen such** devastation?

I **have never seen** anything like it.

1 **What is the island like after the hurricane? Look and match.**

a The hurricane has blown these trees over. _3_
b The wind has blown a car onto the beach. ____
c This house has lost its roof. ____
d The waves have thrown these boats onto the rocks. ____
e A tree has crashed onto this lorry. ____
f The strong winds have smashed these windows. ____

2 **Name these things. You can see them on or near a tropical island.**

Ask and answer.

Have you ever seen a palm tree?   No, I haven't. or Yes, I have.

Now make sentences with *never*.

I have never seen a shark.   Billy has never seen a dolphin.

Turn to Fluency Book 4 Programme 13.

Grammar present perfect with ever/never (Have you ever ...)

Spelling

Can you find the two words in the newspaper on page 109 that end with **or**?
Words that end in **or** are often the names of people who do things.

 doct**or**    sail**or**

Be careful! The **or** at the end of a word often sounds like **er**.

1 Complete each word with *or*. Write the words.
Read the words. Discuss what they mean.

Set A

1 sail _o_ _r_   2 edit __ __   3 act __ __   4 visit __ __   5 profess __ __

sailor   _____   _____   _____   _____

Set B

6 doct __ __   7 auth __ __   8 tail __ __   9 may __ __   10 invent __ __

_____   _____   _____   _____   _____

2 Write the words from *Set A* in alphabetical order.

actor   _____   _____   _____   _____

3 Write the words from *Set B* in alphabetical order.

_____   _____   _____   _____   _____

4 Make up a sentence about each word. Write in your copy book.

Like this: _A professor teaches in a university._

Spelling   *-or suffix*

Class writing

1 **Read the newspaper report on pages 108 and 109 again.**

> Imagine you are a reporter for another newspaper. You have to write a report on the hurricane, too. Do this together as a class.

2 **Think of a good title for your report. It must make people want to read it.**

3 **Write a short paragraph at the beginning of your report to get people interested in the hurricane.**

4 **Write a paragraph about what happened to four different people on the island. Imagine what each person said to you.**

1 Mr Shah a shopkeeper. He lives in the flat above his shop. The wind smashed his shop window and water went everywhere. 	2 Mrs Franks. She was driving home in her car. The wind blew her car off the road. 
3 Mr Parks, the headmaster of the school. Last night people slept in his school gym. 	4 Sally Downs, a nurse. She worked all night at the hospital. 

5 **Discuss what photos you will put in your report.**

> Remember to use direct speech sometimes (see page 111).

Reading for enrichment

Wind

When there is no wind at all,
Flags don't flutter and leaves don't fall.
When there is a gentle breeze,
There's just a rustle in the trees.

When the summer breeze is strong,
Sailing boats are blown along.

When the autumn wind is high,
Leaves and twigs go flying by.

When the winter brings a gale,
Smaller boats should never sail.

When a hurricane comes to town,
Trees and walls come crashing down.

Wind can cool a summer's day
Or wind can blow you right away.

Mike Jubb

Reading extension   poem

Revision 3

1. **Look at the pictures.**
   1. What can you see?
   2. What is the weather like?
   3. Is it raining and windy in your town today?

2. **Listen and read.**

3. **Read and say.**
   Look at picture 1.
   1. Where were Bob and Jim?
   2. What was the weather like?
   3. What was coming?

   Look at picture 2.
   1. Did the wind get better or worse?
   2. Did the waves become bigger or smaller?

   Look at picture 3.
   1. Could they sail the boat?
   2. Why not?

   Look at picture 4.
   1. What happened to Bob and Jim?
   2. Why was Bob frightened?

1 Bob and Jim were sailing in Jim's little boat. Suddenly the sky grew dark. It started to rain and the wind started to blow.

3 They could not sail the boat. The storm was too fierce and the waves were too high. The boat was not big enough. Bob and Jim were not strong enough.

5 Suddenly they heard a noise. A helicopter was flying above them. A man in the helicopter threw down a rope.

2 There was thunder and lightning. The rain poured down. The wind became stronger and stronger. The waves got higher and higher.

4 The boat turned over and the two men fell into the water. Bob could not swim. He was very frightened.

6 Bob went up first and then it was Jim's turn. Soon they were safe inside the helicopter.

Look at picture 5.
1 What did they hear?
2 What did the man throw down?

Look at picture 6.
1 What happened to Bob and Jim?
2 What did Jim say?

4 Finish the sentences.
1 They couldn't sail the boat. The storm was too …
2 They couldn't sail the boat. The waves were too …
3 The boat was not … enough.
4 The men were not … enough.
5 'If the waves get higher, …'
6 'If you catch the rope, …'

5 Listen and say which picture.

6 Act out the story.

unit 14
It's a knockout!

Part 1

Stacey and her twin brother, Steve, were football fans. They played football for their school team, Denston Primary. They talked about football all the time. They watched their favourite team, Denston Rovers, when they played at home.

One evening, Stacey and Steve were watching a football match on TV. Dad was reading the newspaper. Mum came in and sat down. 'Have you finished with the paper, yet?' she asked.

'I've just started reading the sports section,' Dad replied. Suddenly he said, 'Wow! I can't believe it! Look. It says that Brent and Vialli are coming to play football here on Saturday.'

'Really!' Steve said. 'They both play for Italian teams.'

'Why are they coming to play here?' Mum asked.

'Denston Rovers are playing in a special match to raise money for Denston Hospital. They are playing against a team of famous football stars. Brent's family lives here, in Denston, so he is playing in the team. Vialli's his friend,' Dad explained.

'Have you ever seen them play, Dad?' Stacey asked.

'No, I've never seen them,' Dad said, 'but everyone says they're good.'

'Can we go?' Steve asked.

The two children looked at Dad. 'All right,' he said. 'I'll take you.'

Part 2

On Saturday afternoon, the family waited for the match to begin. They were sitting behind one of the goals. The huge crowd cheered as the players ran onto the pitch.

'There they are!' Steve shouted excitedly. He pointed at Brent and Vialli.

The referee blew his whistle. The game started at a very fast pace. It was very exciting.

'Look! Brent's got the ball!' shouted Stacey.

'Now he's passed it to Vialli,' said Steve.

'Shoot!' Dad shouted.

Stimulus   story with familiar setting

Vialli ran towards the goal. A Denston Rovers defender tried to stop him. Vialli ran past the defender easily and kicked the ball at the goal. It missed the goal and zoomed into the crowd like a rocket.

'Look out!' Mum shouted – but it was too late. The ball hit Stacey on the head.

Part 3

'Where am I?' Stacey asked. Dad was sitting next to her. Mum and Steve were standing behind him.

'Don't worry. You're going to be all right,' he said.

'You're in hospital,' Mum said. 'An ambulance brought you here. You were hit on the head by Vialli's shot!'

'I saw the ball coming and then – BANG! I don't remember anything after that,' Stacey said quietly.

A doctor came and examined Stacey. Then Stacey had an X-ray. The doctor brought her back to her family. The family sat around Stacey's bed and waited for the results of the X-ray.

Two hours later, the doctor came back. She smiled at Stacey and said, 'Everything is fine! You're a lucky girl – there are no broken bones.' Stacey and her family were very pleased. 'Oh,' the doctor said. 'There are two men outside who want to see you.'

When the two men walked through the door Stacey was surprised. It was Brent and Vialli. They were still wearing their football kit.

'Are you OK?' Brent asked.

'I'm fine, thank you,' Stacey said quietly.

Then Vialli took something from behind his back and spoke to Brent in Italian. 'Vialli wants to give you a present,' Brent said. Vialli gave Stacey the match ball.

'All the players have signed it for you. It will remind you of today,' Brent said.

'Oh, thank you!' Stacey said excitedly. 'I'm pleased Vialli missed the goal!'

Brent turned to Vialli and translated. Then everyone laughed loudly. 'Vialli thinks you're very funny!' Brent smiled.

Comprehension

1 **Who said it?**

1 'Wow! I can't believe it!'
2 'Can we go?'
3 'Look out!'
4 'I saw the ball coming.'
5 'There are no broken bones.'
6 'Vialli wants to give you a present.'

2 **Discuss your answers to these questions.**

1 How do you know Stacey and Steve both loved football?
2 What do you know about Brent and Vialli?
3 Why is a referee needed in a football match?
4 How do you think Stacey felt when
   a she woke up in hospital?
   b she saw Vialli and Brent in hospital?
   c Vialli gave her a present?

Vocabulary

1 **Match each word with its correct meaning.**

1 fan __c__
2 match ____
3 star ____
4 pitch ____
5 pace ____
6 ball ____
7 kit ____

a a famous actor or sports player
b a round object used in sport
c someone who likes something very much
d special clothes you wear for a sport
e a game in which teams of players compete
f the speed at which something happens
g a flat piece of ground where people play sports

Be careful! Some words have **two meanings**!

2 **Find another meaning for each word above. Use the Dictionary on page 160 to help you. Write the words and the other meanings in your copy book.**

Language building

> **Adverbs** give more meaning to **verbs**.
> An **adverb of place** tells us **where** something happened.
>
> Mum sat **down**.

1 Discuss which word in each sentence is an *adverb of place*. Underline the *adverbs*.

1. Mum came <u>in</u>.
2. Everyone looked up.
3. Dad said, 'Brent is coming to play here.'
4. Mum said, 'Brent's family live nearby.'
5. 'There they are!' Steve shouted.
6. The doctor said, 'There are two men outside.'
7. Brent and Vialli walked away.

2 Here are eight *adverbs of place*. Put them in alphabetical order.

here	1 <u>backwards</u>
there	2 _____
everywhere	3 _____
backwards	4 _____
outside	5 _____
upwards	6 _____
left	7 _____
right	8 _____

3 Make up eight sentences. Use the eight *adverbs of place* in them. Write the sentences in your copy book.

Grammar

Do you remember the story about the football match?

Steve **has just switched on** the TV.

Dad **has just picked up** his newspaper.

'**Have** you **finished** with the paper **yet**?' asks Mum.

'I **haven't finished** with it **yet**,' says Dad.

'I'**ve just started** reading the sports section.'

1 **Ask and answer.**

1

arrived at the stadium?

Have they arrived at the stadium yet?

No, they haven't.

2

bought their tickets?

3

found their seats?

4

match started?

5

scored a goal?

Say and write in your copy book.
Like this: <u>They haven't arrived at the stadium yet.</u>

Remember! haven't = have not

2 **Look and say. Then write.**

1

opened

<u>She has just opened her present.</u>

2

made

3

arrived

4

scored

5

finished

Turn to Fluency Book 4 Programme 14.

122 **Grammar** present perfect + **just** and **yet**

Spelling

Remember!
We can break words into **small parts**. These are **syllables**.
If you say a word **slowly** you can hear how many syllables it has got.
Each syllable must have **one vowel or more**.

tun - nel

See how a **two-syllable word** with a **double consonant** in the middle is split into syllables.

1 Say these words slowly. Can you hear *two syllables* in each word? Discuss what each word means.

> tunnel   apple   pizza   rabbit   yellow
> butter   coffee   mirror   swimmer   lesson

Underline the *double consonant* in the middle of each word.

2 Split each word into *two syllables*.

1 tun + nel = tunnel   2 ___ + ___ = ___
3 ___ + ___ = ___   4 ___ + ___ = ___
5 ___ + ___ = ___   6 ___ + ___ = ___
7 ___ + ___ = ___   8 ___ + ___ = ___
9 ___ + ___ = ___   10 ___ + ___ = ___

3 Match the first and second syllable of each word.

1 tun   a bit _____   6 but   f ror _____
2 ap   b za   _____   7 cof   g son _____
3 piz   c nel tunnel   8 mir   h mer _____
4 rab   d low _____   9 swim   i fee _____
5 yel   e ple _____   10 les   j ter _____

Spelling — two-syllable words with medial double consonants

Class writing

Every story has got a **storyline** or **plot**.
Every story has got a **beginning**, a **middle** and an **end**.
First an author makes a **plan**.
Then the author writes the story.

Look at the story on pages 118 and 119. It has got a clear plan. It is divided into three parts.

1 Write a story plan for 'It's a Knockout.'
Write one or two sentences about each picture.

Part 1

Part 2

Part 3

Writing — planning and writing story sequel

Reading for enrichment

Fascinating football facts

First football club The modern football game started in Britain in 1846. The players made some rules and they had referees to make sure the players did not break the rules. The first football club, Sheffield Football Club, started in 1885.

Can women play football? Women's football is popular. In Britain in 1991 there were 450 women's football clubs. Each week, thousands of women go to watch football, too.

It's a record! A football player in Norway, called Tore Hansen, kicked a ball in the air for four hours! He bounced the ball on his feet, his knees, his shoulders and his head. The ball did not touch the ground!

Youngest and oldest In 1942, Cameron Buchanan played a football game for Wolverhampton Wanderers in Britain. He was fourteen years old! In 1965, Stanley Matthews played his last game for Stoke City. He was fifty years old!

Fog stopped play In 1937, the referee stopped a football match because it was too foggy. The players left the football pitch and got dressed. They could not find their goalkeeper. A policeman looked for him and found him. He was still standing in the goal. He asked where everyone was and why it was so quiet!

A tall story Albert Iremonger played for Notts County in 1900. He was two metres tall! When the players made him angry, he sat on the ball and did not let them play with it!

The Olympic Games

The Olympic Games are the most important athletic competition in the world. What an event! Many athletes from all over the world come to take part in the Games. One billion people watch the Olympic Games on TV.

Some of the sports in the modern Games

- archery
- athletics
- basketball
- beach volleyball
- boxing
- canoeing
- cycling
- equestrianism
- fencing
- gymnastics
- handball
- hockey
- judo
- pentathlon
- rowing
- shooting
- soccer
- swimming

The ancient Olympic Games

The Olympic Games started three thousand years ago in Greece in Olympia. There were races and competitions for men but women could not race. There were running races, wrestling, jumping, throwing spears and racing with chariots. The winners won a prize. Athletes who came second or third, won nothing!

The modern Olympic Games

Baron de Coubertin started thinking about the modern Olympic Games in 1894. He loved sport. He said, 'The important thing in the Olympic Games is not winning but taking part.'

The first new Olympic Games

In 1896, Baron de Coubertin organised the first modern Olympic Games in Athens. Fourteen countries came, and athletes competed in different sports. The Games were very popular. Many people came to watch the athletes.

The Olympic Games now

The Olympic Games take place every four years in countries all over the world. Men and women can now compete in the Games. More countries come now and there are more sports in the competition.

The Olympic flag

The Olympic flag has got five rings. Each ring is a different colour. The rings represent the five continents – Europe, Asia, Africa, America and Australasia. They are joined together to show peace and to show friendly competition.

The Olympic flame

The Olympic Games start with a special celebration. An athlete runs into the stadium. He or she carries a flame and lights the Olympic flame with it.

Some of the 20th century Olympic Games

Year	City	Country	Athletes		Nations	Events
			Men	Women		
1900	Paris	France	1206	19	26	87
1912	Stockholm	Sweden	2490	57	28	102
1924	Paris	France	2956	136	44	126
1948	London	UK	3714	385	59	136
1956	Melbourne	Australia	2958	384	72	151
1964	Tokyo	Japan	4457	683	90	163
1976	Montreal	Canada	4781	1247	92	198
1988	Seoul	South Korea	6279	2186	159	237
1996	Atlanta	USA	6797	3513	197	271

Comprehension

1 **Look at the chart on page 127 and answer these questions.**

1. Where were the Olympic Games held in   a 1912?   b 1956?   c 1976?
2. In which year were there the   a most   b fewest women athletes?
3. In which year did the   a fewest   b most nations take part?
4. In which year were there the   a fewest   b most events?

2 **Discuss your answers to these questions.**

1. How are the ancient and the modern Games different?
2. 'The important thing is not winning but taking part.' Is this true?
3. Can you think of any sports that do *not* appear on pages 126 to 127?
4. What does the Olympic flag represent? Do you like this idea?

Vocabulary

> Remember! It is important to be able to use **alphabetical order**. The words in a **dictionary** or **thesaurus** are in alphabetical order.

1 **Use the first letter of each sport. Put them in alphabetical order.**

| judo   athletics   gymnastics   rowing |

1 _____   2 _____   3 _____   4 _____

2 **Use the second letter of each sport. Put them in alphabetical order.**

| snooker   skating   shooting   squash |

1 _____   2 _____   3 _____   4 _____

3 **Use the third letter of each country. Put them in alphabetical order.**

| Paraguay   Pakistan   Panama |

1 _____   2 _____   3 _____

Language building

A sentence has got a **subject** and a **verb**.
Some sentences also contain an **object**.

This is the **verb**.

The **runner** won a **medal**.

The **subject** is the **main person or thing** in the sentence.

This is the **object**.
An object usually comes **after** a verb.

1 **Underline the *subject* and circle the *verb* in each sentence.**

1 The athlete carried the Olympic flame.
2 The swimmer won the race.
3 The Olympic flag has got five rings.
4 A big crowd filled the stadium.
5 The jumper broke the world record.
6 Thousands of people watched the gymnastics.
7 Baron de Coubertin started the modern Olympic Games.

Discuss what the *object* is in each sentence.

2 **Think of a good *object* for each sentence.**

1 The footballer scored a _____ .
2 The cyclist fell off his _____ .
3 The horse jumped over the _____ .
4 The swimmer dived into the _____ .
5 The athlete threw a _____ .
6 The woman lifted a heavy _____ .
7 My favourite sport is _____ .

Discuss what the *subject* is in each sentence.

Language building   subject and object

Grammar

What do you remember about the Olympic Games?

What an event!

What a wonderful stadium!

What huge crowds!

What excitement!

1 Look at these pictures. Match the sentences to them.

1 _c_ 　2 ___ 　3 ___

4 ___ 　5 ___ 　6 ___

a　What a high jump!
c　What fast runners!
e　How strong he is! What strength!

b　What an excellent shot!
d　What fantastic players!
f　What rough water!

2 Say, then write. Add *What*, *What a* or *What an* to the sentences.

1 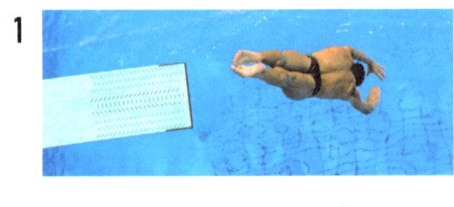　2

_____ perfect dive!　　_____ speed!

3 　4

_____ fantastic athletes!　　_____ interesting flag!

Turn to Fluency Book 4 Programme 15.

130　Grammar　What a...! What an...! What ...!

Spelling

> The **o** in some words sounds like the **u** in s**u**n.
>
> Each ring in the Olympic flag is a different c**o**lour.

1 Read the words.
Underline the **o** that sounds like **u** in each word.

> nothing   money   month   wonderful   son
> love   tongue   colour   front   above

2 Write the words in alphabetical order.

1 _____ 2 _____ 3 _____ 4 _____ 5 _____
6 _____ 7 _____ 8 _____ 9 _____ 10 _____

3 Write the word that means the same.

1 _front_   the opposite of back
2 _____   the opposite of something
3 _____   the opposite of hate
4 _____   the opposite of below
5 _____   the opposite of horrible
6 _____   the male child of a parent
7 _____   the name of the thing that helps you taste
8 _____   red is the name of one
9 _____   January is the name of one
10 _____ something you spend

4 Make up some sentences together.

Use the words you wrote above in your sentences.

Spelling   o sounds like u (nothing)

Class writing

> 1 Draw a chart like the one below.
> 2 Read the information about these swimmers.
> 3 Complete the chart with the information.

The first one has been done for you.

Mark comes from the USA. He entered the 100m breast stroke and the 100m crawl. He won a silver medal in the breast-stroke.

Carl is a Canadian. He won a gold medal for the 100m back-stroke. He was in the 100m breast-stroke but did not win anything in the race.

Dean entered all the races. He won a gold medal in the 100m crawl. He got no other medals. Dean is from Melbourne, in Australia.

Paul is also from Australia. He swam in the 100m breast-stroke but he came last and did not get a medal.

John did very well in the swimming races. He won silver medals for the 100m crawl and the 100m back-stroke. He came fourth in the 100m breast-stroke. John is an American.

Edward was pleased with his results. He won a bronze medal in both the 100m crawl and the 100m breast-stroke. Edward and Paul are twins.

Mike comes from Montreal, in Canada. He entered the 100m breast-stroke and back-stroke races. He came first in the breast-stroke but he came fifth in the back-stroke.

Name	Country			Event			Medals		
	Australia	USA	Canada	100m breast-stroke	100m crawl	100m back-stroke	gold	silver	bronze
Mark		✓		✓	✓			✓	

Reading for enrichment

Dawn Fraser

Dawn Fraser was a famous swimmer. In three Olympics, Dawn Fraser won four gold and four silver medals. This is her story.

Dawn was the youngest child in her family. She had eight brothers and sisters. She was born in Sydney, in Australia. Dawn wanted to learn to swim. When she was a child, Dawn often had asthma and could not breathe very well but this did not stop her. She went to the swimming pool every day and learnt to swim. She practised and practised.

When Dawn was thirteen her brother, Don, died. Before he died, he told Dawn, 'Keep on swimming. One day, you will be a champion.' Dawn always remembered his words.

Dawn moved to Adelaide when she was fifteen. It was a long way from home. She went to a special swimming school. She worked in a shop for some money and swam as much as possible. She won a lot of competitions. In 1956, she swam for Australia in the Melbourne Olympic Games – and won two gold medals! She won a gold medal in the 1960 Rome Olympics, too.

In 1961, Dawn's father died but Dawn continued to work hard to improve her swimming. One night, in 1964, Dawn was driving her mother and sister home. She drove round a corner and hit a lorry. Her mother died in the crash and Dawn injured her back. Dawn was in hospital for nine weeks and was very sad. She thought she could not swim again. But nothing stopped Dawn. Soon she started swimming again. She swam for Australia in the 1964 Tokyo Olympics and won another gold medal! She said that this medal was for her mother and father.

Reading extension — biography

The Martian and the Supermarket

Would you like to find a Martian in a supermarket? Judy did! Read and find out what happened.

It was the middle of the night when the rocket landed in the supermarket car-park. The engine had failed. The hatch opened and the Martian peered out.

A Martian I should tell you, is about three feet high and has webbed feet, green skin and eyes on the ends of horns like a snail. This one, who was three hundred and twenty-seven years old, wore a red jersey.

He said, 'Bother!' He had only passed his driving test the week before and was always losing his way. He was an extremely nervous person, and felt the cold badly. He shivered. A car hooted and he scuttled behind a rubbish bin. Everything looked very strange and frightening.

It began to rain. He wrapped himself in a newspaper, but the rain soon came through that. And then he saw that a sliding door into the back of the supermarket had been left a little bit open, just enough for him to wriggle through.

It was warmer inside, but just as frightening. There were large glass cases that hummed to themselves, and slippery floors, and piles and piles of brightly coloured tins and boxes. He couldn't imagine what it was all for. He curled up between two of the humming cases and went to sleep.

He woke up to find everything brightly lit. He could hear people talking and walking about. He tucked himself as far out of sight as possible. Feet passed him, and silver things on wheels. Once, one with a baby in it stopped just by him. The baby leaned out and saw him and began to cry.

'Ssh...' whispered the Martian. The baby continued to shriek until its mother moved the pram on.

Stimulus fantasy adventure

The Martian couldn't think what he should do. He was hungry and he wanted to go home and the bright lights and loud noises in this place made him jump. He began to cry; tears trickled down his horns. He sniffed, loudly.

It was at this moment that a girl called Judy stopped right beside him. Her mother was hunting for fish fingers in the freezer and Judy was pushing the trolley and also wishing she could go home; she hated shopping. She heard a peculiar fizzing noise come from the gap between the fishfingers freezer and the one beside it, and looked in.

Plenty of people, looking between two freezers in a supermarket and seeing a thing there like a three-foot green snail with a red jersey on would have screamed. Or fainted. I think I would have. Not so Judy. She bent down for a closer look.

'Please don't tell anyone,' said the Martian. 'They might be unkind to me.'

'Are you a boy or a girl?' asked Judy.

'I'm not sure. Does it matter?'

'Sometimes,' said Judy, after a moment's thought. 'It depends how you're feeling.' She studied the Martian with care. 'I think you're a boy. It's something about your eyes. Never mind. Some boys I quite like. How did you get here?'

'My rocket went wrong and I'd lost the map. Do you think you could help me get away?'

Judy thought about this. 'I would if I could.'

'I don't want to stay here,' – the Martian's voice shook – 'All these people make me nervous and the noise gives me a headache.'

Judy looked round. Her mother had met a friend and was busy chatting. 'Tell you what,' she said. 'Come home with us and I'll think of something.'

'Will it be all right?' said the Martian doubtfully.

'I don't know,' said Judy. 'But let's try it anyway and see. Quick – get into this box.' Her mother had put a cardboard box into the trolley, ready to stack the shopping in. Judy looked round again – her mother was still chatting – grabbed the Martian, bundled him into the box and shut the flaps.

Comprehension

1 **Think of an ending for each sentence.**

1. The rocket landed in …
2. A Martian is about three feet high and has …
3. When a car hooted, the Martian …
4. The Martian went to sleep between …
5. The baby saw him and …

2 **Discuss your answers to these questions.**

1. Why did the Martian land in the supermarket car park?
2. What can we learn about the Martian from the story?
3. Why did everything look 'strange and frightening' to the Martian?
4. Do you feel sorry for the Martian?
5. Imagine there is a Martian in your supermarket. What do you do?

Vocabulary

We can use lots of different verbs which mean **to speak**.

1 **Complete these 'speaking' verbs from the story.**

1 s a i d   2 _sk_d   3 wh_sp_r_d

2 **Write a *verb* that means the same. Use the Thesaurus on page 167.**

1 yelled _____   2 murmured _____

3 moaned _____   4 replied   _____

5 sobbed _____

3 **Think of a suitable speaking word for each sentence.**

1. 'I hate shopping!' … Judy.
2. 'I'm f-f-f-freezing,' … the Martian.
3. 'Quick! No-one is looking. Get in here!' … Judy.
4. 'What are you doing?' Judy's Mum … .

Language building

16

> Remember! An **adjective** is a **describing** word that tells us more about a **noun**.
>
> A **possessive adjective** tells us who **possesses** (or owns) something. **His** tells you more about the jersey.
>
> The Martian wore a **red** jersey. **His** jersey was red.

Here are some possessive adjectives: | my your his her our its their

1 Find and circle the *possessive adjective* in each snake.

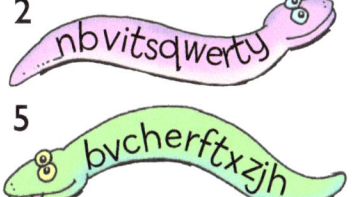
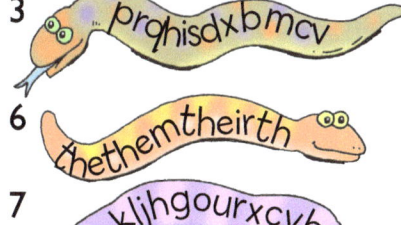

2 Underline the *possessive adjective* in each sentence.

1. The Martian was three feet high and his skin was green.
2. The rocket landed and its door opened.
3. 'I've lost my map,' the Martian said.
4. 'What's your name?' Judy asked the Martian.
5. Judy took the Martian to her house.
6. The Martian said to Judy, 'Don't tell anyone our secret.'
7. Judy and Mum got into their car.

3 Discuss which is the correct *possessive adjective* for each gap.

1. Mum was chatting to (his/her) friend.
2. The shop was shut but (its/my) back door was open.
3. The Martian asked Judy, 'Are you with (our/your) mother?'
4. Judy pointed to Mum and said, '(Her/My) mother is there.'
5. Judy said to Mum, '(Its/Our) shopping is very heavy.'
6. The Martian cried and tears trickled down (his/her) horns.
7. Mum and Judy ate (our/their) dinner.

Language building possessive adjectives

Grammar

Do you remember the Martian in the supermarket?

Would you like some help?

How about coming home with me?

What about jumping into this box?

Shall we try it?   **Let's** try it and see.

1 Make suggestions to the Martian. Use: **Shall we …?**   **Let's …**

1
go to my house

2
get something to eat

3
have a drink

4
watch TV

2 Make more suggestions. Use: **How about …?**   **What about …?**

1
go for a walk

2
play basketball

3
have a picnic

4
buy an ice cream

3 Read. Make suggestions. Answer.

You are in the supermarket with your mum and your friend. Your mum says you can choose the food for a picnic.

> sandwiches   chicken   grapes   bananas   biscuits   cakes

Would you like some…?

Shall we/Let's get some…?

How/What about getting some…?

OK!

All right!

Yes, please!

Good idea!

Turn to Fluency Book 4 Programme 16.

138   *Grammar*   making offers and suggestions

Spelling

> **Remember!**
> We can break words into **small parts**. These are **syllables**.
> If you say a word **slowly** you can hear how many syllables it has got.
> Each syllable must have **one vowel or more**.
>
> This word has got **three** syllables.
>
> frigh + ten + ing = frightening

1 Do these *syllable* sums.

1 im + por + tant = __important__   2 hos + pit + al = _____
3 pop + u + lar = _____   4 ex + pen + sive = _____
5 dif + fer + ent = _____   6 news + pa + per = _____
7 sud + den + ly = _____   8 ad + ven + ture = _____
9 to + geth + er = _____   10 bas + ket + ball = _____

Discuss the meaning of each word.

2 Use the correct word to complete each sentence.

1 The doctor worked in the __hospital__.
2 _____ is the name of a sport.
3 Our new car was very _____ .
4 My friend and I went to the shops _____ .
5 I like to read the _____ .
6 Red is the most _____ colour.
7 _____ a rocket landed in the supermarket car park.
8 The king was a very _____ person.
9 Judy had an exciting _____ at the supermarket.
10 The Martian's jersey was a _____ colour from mine.

Spelling   three-syllable words

Class writing

1 In stories we learn a lot from *what people say*.

Imagine that the story continues like this:

> Mum and Judy carried the shopping indoors.
> 'This box is very heavy!' Judy's mum said.
> Judy did not reply. She put the shopping on the kitchen table.
> 'Shall we unpack the shopping?' Judy's mum asked.
> 'Let's have a cup of tea first,' Judy replied.
> 'No. I want to put the shopping away,' her mum said.
> She opened the cardboard box …

1. What can we learn from the things Judy and her mother say?
2. What do you think Mum will say next? What will she do?
3. What do you think Judy will say? What will she do?
4. What do you think the Martian will say? What will he do?

> Judy's Mum says the Martian can stay.
> Judy takes him to school with her. …

5. What will her friends say?
6. What will the teacher say?
7. What will happen?

2 Discuss your ideas. Continue the story together as a class.

Remember to include a lot of **conversation** (the things people say).

Reading for enrichment

> Has anyone ever laughed at you? How did you feel?

The professor and the ferryman

There was an old man who rowed people across a deep river in his boat. The ferryman was not rich; he was not clever; he could not read or write; but he was happy. He liked his job. He was never in a hurry and he liked to think.

One day a very smart man wanted to cross the river. He was carrying a briefcase and was very important. He asked the old man to row him across the river. The smart man got into the boat and sat down. In the middle of the river, he spoke to the ferryman. He said, 'Have you studied science?'

The ferryman replied, 'No, Sir. I haven't studied science. I haven't been to school and I haven't learnt to read or write.'

The man was very surprised. 'You haven't studied science! I am an important professor. I know about science! I teach science at the university.'

The ferryman was sad. He felt stupid. He did not think he was important. He rowed boats. He wasn't clever like the professor.

Suddenly, some dark clouds appeared in the sky. A strong wind blew. The water got rougher and rougher and the boat started to rock. The wind got stronger and stronger. The waves on the river got bigger and bigger. The boat started to sink. 'Swim!' the ferryman shouted.

The professor was frightened. 'I can't swim!' he shouted.

A big wave knocked the men into the water. The professor shouted and waved his arms in the air. He started to sink under the water. The old man grabbed the professor and swam to the side of the river. He crawled onto the riverbank and pulled the professor out of the water.

'How can I thank you?' the professor said. 'I thought I was a clever man, but how did it help me?'

Reading extension — story with a moral

The visit

Some animals are endangered. They are in danger. There are not many of them left in the world. If they die out, they will become extinct. Would you like these animals to disappear? Lizzie saw some endangered animals on a school visit to the zoo.

Last week, Mrs Mills took my class on a visit to the zoo. Some of our parents came. We brought sandwiches and also took some drinks with us. On the journey to the zoo we laughed and sang. Everyone was very excited.

We soon arrived. The zoo was huge. There were high fences around the animals but they had lots of space to move around.

Mrs Mills told us that most of the animals were rescued when their mothers were killed. She told us that some of the animals, like the tiger, were endangered. Mrs Mills said that the zoo was trying to help these rare animals to breed and have babies.

We saw the chimpanzees first. They had long arms. They were very comical. Some chimpanzees chased each other up and down the trees. They loved climbing and swinging. Some picked things out of their fur. Mrs Mills said they were grooming. Some chimpanzees were cracking peanut shells and eating the nuts. Mrs Mills told us that people catch chimpanzees and use them for medical experiments and research.

Next, we walked over a bridge and saw lots of crocodiles in a pond. Mrs Mills explained that people use crocodile skin to make shoes and handbags and that some parts of crocodiles are used to make perfume. Some crocodiles were sleeping in the sun on the bank. My eyes are blue. Theirs are black. I didn't like them. The crocodiles' teeth were very sharp. I was glad when we went to see the tigers!

The zookeeper was feeding the tigers. He threw some raw meat to them. Two tigers wanted the same piece of meat and growled at each other. They were very fierce. One tiger was lying on a branch of a tree. It was difficult to see him. His stripy coat was good camouflage. The zookeeper said that some people hunted tigers and made rugs and coats from their fur.

Soon it was lunchtime. We sat on the grass, near several elephants. They were enormous. Their skin was very wrinkled and dusty. They picked up things to eat with their trunks and put them in their mouths. They flapped their big ears all the time. We learnt that hunters kill many elephants. The hunters want their tusks. The tusks are made of a bone called ivory. People use it to make ornaments and jewellery.

Mrs Mills sat with her back to the elephants. A big elephant came to the fence. It reached over and took Mrs Mills' sun hat off her head with its trunk! The elephant waved the hat backwards and forwards, and then it tried to eat it!

After lunch, it was time to go home. The zookeeper gave us a worksheet to do at school. What a lovely visit!

Comprehension

1 Number the sentences in the correct order.

___ We soon arrived. Some chimpanzees chased each other.

_1_ On the journey to the zoo we laughed and sang all the way.

___ We sat on the grass, near several elephants.

___ Next, we walked over a bridge and saw lots of crocodiles in a pond.

___ An elephant reached over and took Mrs Mills' sun hat off her head.

___ A tiger was lying on a branch of a tree.

2 Discuss your answers to these questions.
1. Is it important for animals to have lots of space in a zoo?
2. Why did the zoo contain endangered animals?
3. Why do people hunt and kill the different animals in the zoo?
4. Which animals do you think Lizzie liked best? Why?

Vocabulary

Use the Thesaurus on page 167 to help.

1 Find a word with the correct number of letters and the same meaning.

1. raw _____
2. sharp _____
3. wrinkled _____
4. comical _____
5. fierce _____
6. glad _____
7. extinct _____
8. excited _____

*Some words have got **antonyms** (words that mean the **opposite**).*

2 Choose the correct *antonym* for each word.

1. raw _____
2. sharp _____
3. wrinkled _____
4. comical _____
5. glad _____
6. fierce _____
7. extinct _____
8. excited _____

sad	blunt
tame	smooth
miserable	bored
cooked	alive

Language building

Do you remember what a **possessive noun** is?
In Unit 8 we learnt about **singular** possessive nouns.

A **possessive noun** tells us who **owns** something.
It tells us who something **belongs to**.

If the noun is **plural** (there is **more than one** owner):

- we add **'** to the noun if it ends with **s**.

the monkeys' tails
(The tails belong to the monkeys.)

- we add **'s** if the noun does **not** end with **s**.

the children**'s** hats
(The hats belong to the children.)

1 *Who owns the underlined nouns?*

1. The lions' <u>den</u> is in the forest.   <u>the lions</u>
2. The monkeys' <u>tails</u> are long.   _____
3. The tigers' <u>stripes</u> are black.   _____
4. The elephants' <u>trunks</u> are wrinkled.   _____
5. The chimpanzees' <u>arms</u> were long.   _____
6. The ants' <u>nest</u> was under a rock.   _____

Are the owners *singular* or *plural*? How can you tell?

2 *Write sentences.*

1. the oxen's cart   <u>The cart belongs to the oxen.</u>
2. the men's coats   _____
3. the women's bags   _____
4. the mice's cheese   _____
5. the children's books   _____
6. the staff's car park   _____
7. the geese's eggs   _____

Language building   apostrophes of possession (plural)

Grammar

Do you remember Lizzie's visit to the zoo?

We enjoyed **visiting** the zoo.

We liked **watching** the chimpanzees.

The chimpanzees loved **swinging**.

They were good at **climbing**, too.

We were interested in **watching** the animals.

1 Find the correct ending.

1. The chimpanzees were
2. I didn't like
3. We loved
4. The zoo keepers like

a watching the tigers.
b working with animals.
c standing near crocodiles.
d good at climbing.

2 Guess the animal.

 It likes eating grass.
Yes, it is.

Is it the horse?

Use these words: likes   loves   enjoys   is good at

Hello!

3 What about you? Ask your friends. Then write in your copy book.

What do you enjoy/love doing?
What are you good at doing?

Turn to Fluency Book 4 Programme 17.

Spelling

> The letters **al** often come at the **beginning** of words.
> The letters **al** often come at the **end** of words, too.
>
> Can you find any words that **begin** or **end** with **al** on pages 142 and 143?
>
> There were sever**al** anim**al**s in the zoo.

1 Make these words. Read the words you make.

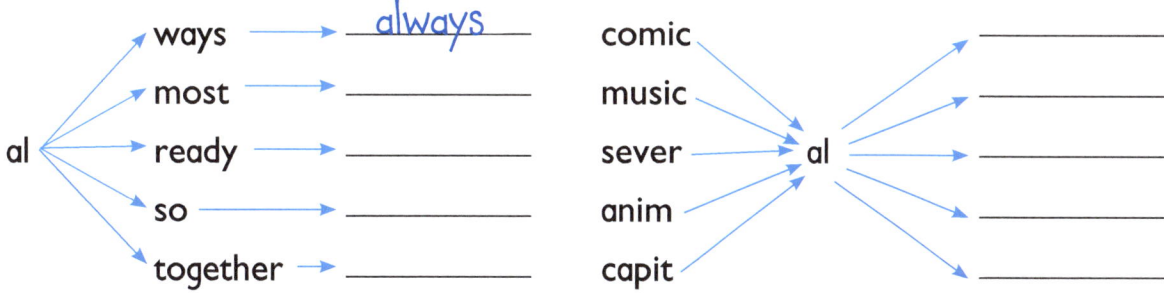

al → ways → *always*
   → most → _____
   → ready → _____
   → so → _____
   → together → _____

comic → _____
music → _____
sever → al → _____
anim → _____
capit → _____

2 Discuss which is the best word to complete each sentence.

1 It will soon be my brother's birthday. He is ... four.
2 Cairo is the ... of Egypt.
3 An elephant is a big ... . A giraffe is ... a big animal.
4 I am ... happy.
5 Fifty and fifty make one hundred ... .
6 I like music. I am very ... .
7 Chimpanzees are very funny. They are very ... .
8 I have ... finished my sandwiches.
9 I have ... books in my bag.

3 Look carefully at the words that *begin* with *al*.

4 Look carefully at the words that *end* with *al*.

> Now close your book. Spell the words in your copy book. Do not copy!

Spelling   *al* as prefix and suffix

Class writing

On pages 142 and 143, Lizzie wrote about her visit to the zoo.
She told us about what she saw and what she did.
This sort of writing is called a **recount**.
She tried to make it interesting.

1 Think of something you have done together as a class. Did you:

- see a film?
  - have a special visitor?
    - have a party?
      - go on a visit?
        - perform a play?
          - do something else?

2 Choose an event and write a class recount of it together.

Here are some ideas to help you think. Discuss your ideas.

- When did it happen?
  - Where did it take place?
    - Who went?
      - How did you get to the place?
        - Did you have to take anything?
          - How did you feel before you went?
        - What did you think when you first arrived?
      - What did you see?
    - What happened?
  - Did anything unusual or funny happen?
- How did you feel when it finished?

Look back at the recount on pages 142 and 143. Notice that Lizzie wrote in **paragraphs**. Try to make your recount as interesting as possible.

Reading for enrichment

Endangered animals

Chimpanzee 	**Lives:** West Africa **Hunted for:** pets and zoos; medical research **Facts:** There are 50,000 chimpanzees living in the jungle. Many chimpanzees die when they are moved to a different place.
Tiger 	**Lives:** India, South and Eastern Asia, Siberia **Hunted for:** fur for making coats and rugs; bones for medicines **Facts:** There were eight different tigers. Two are extinct and there aren't many of the other ones. In 1970 India started *Project Tiger* to help save the tiger.
African elephant 	**Lives:** Central and Southern Africa **Hunted for:** Ivory tusks to make ornaments and jewellery **Facts:** A lot of elephants are killed every year. There are fewer than 600,000 elephants in the world.
Arabian oryx 	**Lives:** Middle East **Hunted for:** sport **Facts:** This animal disappeared in the wild in 1970. In 1980, a zoo released some oryx. The zoo put them back in the wild. The local people protect them carefully.
Crocodile 	**Lives:** Central America, Central and Southern Africa, Southern Asia **Hunted for:** skin to make shoes, bags, leather items **Facts:** Crocodiles do not have many babies. Crocodiles are protected and now there are more of them.

unit 18

What is a friend?

> We all have the gift of friendship. It is precious – like a jewel!
> Do you give yours to other people or keep it to yourself?

What is a friend?

A friend is someone who:

Forgives you when you are unkind.
Respects you always.
Includes you in every game.
Encourages you when you are sad.
Never hurts you.
Discusses secret things with you.

A smile

A smile is such a lovely thing
It brightens up your face
And when it's gone it's hard to find
Its secret hiding place.

Yet still more wonderful it is
To know what smiles can do.
You smile at me. I smile at you
And then one smile makes two.

Anon.

150 Stimulus   poems (including an acrostic poem)

Remember me?

Remember me?
I am the boy who sought your friendship;
The boy you turned away.
I am the boy who asked you
If I too might play.
I am the face at the window
When your party was inside,
I am the lonely figure
That walked away and cried.
I am the one who hung around,
A punchbag for your games.
Someone you could kick and beat,
Someone to call names.

But how strange is the change
After time has hurried by.
Four years have passed since then
Now I'm not so quick to cry.
I'm bigger and I'm stronger,
I've grown a foot in height.
Suddenly I'M popular
And YOU'RE left out the light.
I could, if I wanted,
Be so unkind to you.
I would only have to say
And the other boys would do.
But the memory of my pain
Holds back the revenge I'd planned
And instead, I feel much stronger
By offering you my hand.

Ray Mather

Comprehension

1 **Answer these questions about the two poems on page 150.**

1. In the first poem, what does the first letter of each line spell, when you read the letters from top to bottom?
2. When does a friend
   a forgive you?   b respect you?   c encourage you?   d hurt you?
3. What does a friend discuss with you?
4. When a smile has gone, what is it hard to find?
5. How can one smile make two?

2 **Discuss the following things about the *Remember me?* poem.**

1. Name some bad things that happened to the writer in the first verse.
2. In the first verse, how do you feel about
   a the writer of the poem?   b the boy he is talking to?
3. In what ways has the writer of the poem changed in verse 2?
4. In what ways has the boy he is talking to changed in verse 2?
5. There is an old saying: 'He who forgives, gains the victory'. What do you think this means? Do you think it is true?

Vocabulary

Some poems **rhyme**. Rhyming words contain the **same sound**.
Sometimes the words contain the **same letter pattern**, e.g. f**ace**, pl**ace**.
Sometimes the letter patterns are **different**, e.g. ins**ide**, cr**ied**.

1 **Say the words. Match and write the pairs of rhyming words. Which words contain the *same letter patterns*?**

1 face _b_   a play   _____
2 do ____   b place   _face, place_
3 away ____   c cry   _____
4 inside ____   d two   _____
5 by ____   e hand   _____
6 height ____   f cried   _____
7 planned ____ g light   _____

Now think of another word that rhymes with each pair of words.

Language building

Remember! **A pronoun** can be used **in the place of a noun**.

A smile is such a lovely thing
It [a smile] brightens up your face.

A possessive pronoun shows **ownership** or **possession**.

I have a computer. The computer is **mine**.

Here are some possessive pronouns:

> mine   yours   his   hers   ours   theirs

1 **Underline the *possessive pronoun* in each sentence.**

1 This book is mine.
2 My bag is blue – yours is red.
3 The boy was sure the pen was his.
4 Sam pointed to Anna and said, 'This ruler is hers.'
5 Rex belonged to the children – the dog was theirs.
6. 'You can't have the ball. It's ours!' Tom and Ben shouted.

2 **Use *possessive pronouns* in place of the underlined words.**

1 'The toy Ali broke was our toy (ours)!' Amy and Emma complained.
2 The girl picked up the purse – it was her purse (_____).
3 Mr Smith drove a sports car but it was not his car. (_____).
4 The silver bike is my bike (_____).
5 'I think these socks are your socks (_____)!' Mum said to John.
6 Mr and Mrs Lee have got a big car but my car is bigger than their car (_____).

Grammar

Do you remember the poems about friendship?

A friend is someone **who** forgives you when you are unkind.

A friend is someone **who** respects you always.

A friend is someone **who** includes you in every game.

A friend is someone **who** never hurts you.

1 Write *true* or *false*.

1. A doctor is someone who works in a library.   *false*
2. A teacher is someone who works in a school.   _____
3. A pilot is someone who drives lorries.   _____
4. A baker is someone who sells meat.   _____
5. A shepherd is someone who looks after sheep.   _____
6. A clown is someone who makes you cry.   _____

How many sentences were false? Correct them.

2 Work with a friend. Finish the sentences.

1. A librarian is someone who _____
2. A chef _____
3. A nurse _____

3 Think about a friend. Write three sentences.

Start like this:

My friend is someone who ...

Turn to Fluency Book 4 Programme 18.

Grammar — relative clauses (**who**)

Spelling

The letters **el** sometimes come at the end of a word.

a cam**el**

1 Complete each word with *el*. Write each word.
Read the words. Discuss the meaning of each word.

 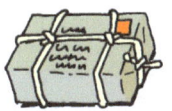  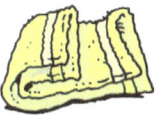 

cam _e l_   parc ___   jew ___   tow ___   hot ___

_____   _____   _____   _____   _____

vow ___   lab ___   trav ___   tunn ___   squirr ___

_____   _____   _____   _____   _____

2 Match each word with its meaning.

1 camel _c_   a a precious stone
2 parcel ___   b Each of these letters: a, e, i, o, u, is a ...!
3 jewel ___   c This animal lives in the desert.
4 towel ___   d to move from one place to another place
5 hotel ___   e something you wrap in special paper
6 vowel ___   f You use this to dry your hands.
7 label ___   g a small animal with a thick tail that lives in a tree
8 travel ___   h a long hole under the ground or through a hill
9 tunnel ___   i a building where you pay to stay in a room
10 squirrel ___   j a piece of paper you put on something

3 Find and write ten words that end with *el*.

1 w j e e l   _jewel_   2 t h e o l   _____
3 m a l e c   _____   4 l o t w e   _____
5 r a c e l p _____   6 b a l l e   _____
7 n u t n l e _____   8 e w l o v   _____
9 t a r e l v _____   10 q u e r l i s r _____

Spelling *el* words

Class writing

The poem, *What is a friend*, on page 150 is called an **acrostic poem**.
The first letter of each line spells the word **friend**.
Acrostic poems do not have to rhyme.

1 **Read this *acrostic poem* that Tom wrote about happiness.**

Happiness is:
Having a good friend
Always smiling
Playing on my computer
Parties
Ice creams
Nice clothes
Eating pizzas
Sunny days
Singing songs

2 **Write a class *acrostic poem* about happiness.**

> Brainstorm lots of ideas for each letter
> and write them on the board.
> Choose which ideas you like best.
> Then make them into your **acrostic poem**.

Reading for enrichment

If we want the world to be a better place, we must be kind to people and we must be kind to the world.

The World with its Countries

The world with its countries,
Mountains and seas,
People and creatures,
Flowers and trees,
The fish in the waters,
The birds in the air
Are calling to ask us
All to take care.

These are our treasures,
A gift from above,
We should say thank you
With a care that shows love
For the blue of the ocean,
The clearness of air,
The wonder of forests
And the valleys so fair.

The song of the skylark,
The warmth of the sun,
The rushing of clear streams
And new life begun
Are gifts we should cherish,
So join in the call
To strive to preserve them
For the future of all.

John Cotton

 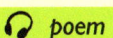

Revision 4

1 Look at the pictures.
1 Who is Mark talking about?
2 Who are your favourite people?

2 Listen and read.

3 Read and say.
Look at picture 1.
1 Describe Mark.
2 How old do you think he is?

Look at picture 2.
1 Who is Danny?
2 What does he like doing?
3 Does he always tell good jokes?

Look at picture 3.
1 Who is this?
2 What is his job?
3 Why does Mark like him?

Look at picture 4.
1 Who are these children?
2 Why does Mark love visiting them?

1
Hi! My name's Mark. Let me introduce you to some of my favourite people.

3 This is Uncle Leo. He's a pilot. He phones me when he's in town.

Hi, Mark! Have you finished your homework yet? How about going for a ride in my new car?

5
This is Harvey Benson. He's my favourite sportsman. He's a fantastic runner. He won a gold medal at the last Olympic Games. He's the kind of person who always does his best. He always tries really hard. I've just found this picture of him in a magazine.

2 This is my best friend, Danny. He's great. He likes telling jokes.

4 These are my cousins, Lily and Alex. They live at the seaside. I love visiting them in the summer. Alex is a great swimmer and Lily enjoys sailing.

3 Is Alex good at swimming?
4 What does Lily enjoy doing?

Look at picture 5.
1 Who is this man?
2 What does he do?
3 Why does Mark like him?

4 **Make sentences.**
What are these people good at?
- Danny
- Uncle Leo
- Lily
- Alex
- Harvey Benson

5 **Listen. Who is speaking?**

6 **Make up a short conversation between Mark and one of his favourite people.
Act it out!**

159

Dictionary

address	the name of the place where you live, including the house number, street, area and town
African	something or someone from Africa
airfield	a small airport for aircraft
amphibian	an animal which lives on land but lays its eggs in water
ancient	very old
arguing	disagreeing
arrived	reached a place
athlete	someone who is good at sports
attacked	fought
author	someone who writes books
awaken	to wake up
ball	1 a round object used in sport 2 special dance, usually with a meal
Baobab	a tree that grows in Africa
bamboo	a type of tall grass which grows in tropical areas
blocks	stops something getting by
blow	move the air
bodies	plural of body – the trunk or main part of a living creature
breed	to have babies; to become parents of young animals
bundled	made someone go in a particular place by pushing them
burn	to make very hot; set on fire
burning	1 being damaged by fire 2 looking like fire
calm	peaceful; very little wind
camel	a large desert mammal with one or two humps
camouflage	colours that hide animals by making them look like the natural background
carries	moves something from place to place
castle	a large strong building from the past, with thick walls
celebrate	to do something enjoyable in order to show that an occasion or event is special
cellar	a room under a building, below ground

cello	musical instrument with strings like a large violin
character	a person in a play, story, etc.
coat	a piece of clothing with long sleeves worn over other clothes
cockpit	the place where the pilot sits in an aeroplane
colonies	groups of animals that live together
comical	funny
compete	to try to win a competition
cradle	a bed for a baby
curved	a shape like an arch
cyclone	another word for a hurricane
damaged	harmed
deep	a long way down from the top of something
delicious	having a pleasant taste or smell
destruction	severe damage
devastation	serious damage and destruction
dormant	asleep
drain	letting liquid flow out
dry	opposite of wet
dusty	covered in dust
editor	someone in charge of a newspaper or magazine
encourages	gives someone confidence and hope
endangered	at risk, in danger
engine	the part of a vehicle that makes it move
engineer	someone who makes or mends engines
erupts	explodes
escape	get free
event	something that happens in a sports competition
explode	burst with a lot of force and a loud noise
extinct	dead, finished
extremely	very
fan	1 someone who likes something very much
	2 something you wave in front of your face to make you cool
fence	a flat, upright structure made of wire or wood, that surrounds an area of land
ferocious	fierce

foot	a measure which equals about 30 centimetres	**hard**	not easy to break
forgives	decides to stop being angry with someone who has done something that is bad	**hatch**	a door
		heavy	with a lot of weight
		horse	a large strong mammal that is used for riding and pulling carts and heavy loads
fresh	new	**hospital**	a place where ill or injured people get help
friendly	kind and helpful		
furry	covered with fur	**hurricane**	a violent storm with extremely strong winds and heavy rain
gale	a very strong wind		
gap	a space between two things	**hurried**	moved quickly
		imaginary	not real
gazed	looked at for a long time	**important**	of great interest or value
gemstone	a valuable stone used in jewellery	**injured**	hurt
		inventor	someone who invents things
germs	bacteria that spread disease	**jockey**	someone whose job it is to ride horses in races
gigantic	extremely large		
glinted	sparkled		
good	enjoyable		
grain	seeds from cereal plants	**journey**	travelling from one place to another
		kit	1 special clothes you wear for a sport
grassland	a large area of land where wild grass grows		2 a set of equipment for a particular activity, e.g. a tool kit
grooming	cleaning itself or another animal		
guarding	protecting a place or person	**knockout**	a hit that knocks someone down

know	to be certain about	**nervous**	worried and slightly afraid
lava	hot, liquid rock flowing out of a volcano	**no**	opposite of yes
lazy	not willing to work	**oiled**	covered with a thin layer of oil
learnt	gained knowledge	**pace**	1 the speed at which something happens
lion	a large African wild cat with yellow fur		2 a step that you take
locked	fastened with a key	**palm**	1 the inside part of the hand
lonely	unhappy because you are alone		
long	not short		2 a type of tree
magma	hot, liquid rock inside a volcano		
mammal	warm-blooded animal	**peculiar**	strange
Martian	a being from Mars	**peered**	looked
marvellous	very good	**piccolo**	a musical instrument like a small flute
match	1 a game in which teams of players compete against each other	**pilot**	someone who flies an aircraft
		pitch	1 a flat piece of ground for playing sports on
	2 a small wooden stick that lights with a flame		2 to throw something
		plane	a short word for aeroplane
mayor	an important official in a town or city	**pride**	a group of lions
modern	very new	**professor**	a clever, highly educated person, who often teaches at a university
mountains	very high hills		
narrator	someone who tells the story		
nation	a country	**prop**	an object that is used in a play or film

protect	to keep someone or something safe		because they have hurt you in the past
punchbag	a stuffed bag for punching (a boxer uses a punchbag for practice)	**right**	1 correct
			2 opposite of left
		roaring	making a loud, deep sound
rare	not often seen or found	**Rra**	a polite way to speak to an older person in Africa
raw	uncooked		
recipe	instructions for making something to eat	**sailor**	someone who travels in a boat on the water
referee	someone who makes sure the players in a game do not break the rules	**saucepan**	a round, deep container with a handle used for cooking
remember	to have a picture in your mind of something that happened in the past	**saw**	1 past tense of the verb 'to see'
			2 a tool that is used for cutting wood or metal
repair	mend		
reply	to say, write or do something as an answer	**scenery**	the furniture and painted background of a theatre stage
		scratchy	itchy
reptile	an animal whose body is covered in scales	**scuttled**	ran away quickly
research	the study of something to discover some new facts	**sea**	a large area of salt water
		secretary	someone in an office who does jobs for someone else such as arranging meetings, making phone calls and preparing letters
respects	treats someone in a way that shows you think they are important		
restaurant	an eating place		
revenge	something that you do to hurt someone	**see**	use your eyes

setting	the time or place in which the events of a play or story, etc. happen	**sprang**	jumped quickly
several	many, lots of	**sprinkle**	scatter
sew	use a needle and thread	**stadium**	a large building (usually without a roof) for sports events
shade	area not in sunlight	**star**	1 a famous actor or sports player
shady	out of the sun		2 a small bright light in the sky at night
shape	to make something they way you want it to look	**starfish**	a small flat sea animal shaped like a star
shriek	to cry loudly	**stove**	a cooker
sighed	breathed out to make a long, slow sound		
skimmed	to move quickly just above something	**strong**	powerful
slice	a piece of food that has been cut from a larger piece	**storm**	strong winds with rain and perhaps thunder
		succeed	to achieve something that you planned to do or attempted to do
slunk	moved in a sly way	**suggested**	offered an idea or plan for something
snail	a small animal with a soft body and a hard shell. Snails move very slowly	**suitcase**	a large bag with a handle used for carrying clothes when you travel
snarled	made an unpleasant, angry sound	**sunshine**	light from the sun
so	very	**tailor**	someone who makes clothes
sobbed	cried noisily	**tiny**	very small
sought	looked for	**tire**	to become tired

to	1 used with verbs (*to be*, *to run*, etc.)	**vegetable**	a part of a plant used as food
	2 used to relate one part of a sentence to another (*Mary went to school.*)	**vent**	a hole in the top of a volcano
		violent	forceful; hard to control
tongue	a long piece of soft flesh that is fixed to the bottom of the mouth	**volcano**	an opening in the Earth where hot liquid and ash are pushed out
tortoise	an animal with a shell on its back	**wailing**	crying with a long, high sound, as if you are in pain or very sad
too	as well as; also	**watched**	looked at something for a long time
translate	to change words into another language	**weather**	what it is like outside, e.g. hot, cold, windy
tune	a song	**webbed**	to have skin between the toes
turkey	a large bird like a chicken		
		wild	not tame
two	a number which comes after 'one'	**wrapping**	going around something
tyre	a thick rubber cover that fits around a wheel	**wreck**	something that has been damaged
		wrestle	to try to push or throw someone to the ground
umpire	someone whose job it is to see players follow the rules of the game	**wrinkled**	lined, creased
		write	use a pen or pencil to make letters or numbers on paper
valley	a low area of land between two mountains or hills	**zoomed**	moved with great speed and energy

Thesaurus

centre	middle (opposite: **edge**)
cold	cool, chilly, bitter, crisp, icy (opposite: **hot**)
comical	funny, humorous, amusing (opposite: **sad**)
cyclone	hurricane
excited	thrilled (opposite: **bored**)
extinct	dead, finished (opposite: **alive**)
fierce	wild, dangerous (opposite: **tame**)
gentle	tender (opposite: **rough**)
glad	pleased, happy, delighted (opposite: **miserable**)
lazy	idle, slow (opposite: **active**)
lift	raise (opposite: **lower**)
moaned	complained, grumbled (opposite: **rejoiced**)
murmured	whispered (opposite: **shouted**)
raw	uncooked, fresh (opposite: **cooked**)
replied	answered (opposite: **asked**)
scared	frightened
scream	yell, shriek
shady	cloudy, dim (opposite: **sunlit**)
sharp	pointed (opposite: **blunt**)
shed	hut
sobbed	cried, wept
strong	powerful (opposite: **weak**)
sunny	fine, bright (opposite: **cloudy**)
wrinkled	lined, creased (opposite: **smooth**)
yelled	shouted loudly (opposite: **whispered**)

Macmillan Education Limited
4 Crinan Street
London N1 9XW

Companies and representatives throughout the world

ISBN 978-1-405-08125-2

Text © Mary Bowen, Louis Fidge, Liz Hocking, Wendy Wren 2006
Design and illustration © Macmillan Education Limited 2006

The authors have asserted their right to be identified as the authors of this work in accordance with the Copyright, Designs and Patents Act 1988.

First published 2006

All rights reserved. No part of this publication may be reproduced, stored in a retrieval system, or transmitted in any form or by any means, electronic, mechanical, photocopying, recording, or otherwise, without the prior written permission of the publishers.

Original design by Wild Apple Design Ltd
Page make-up by Cambridge Publishing Management Limited
Illustrated by Carlos Avalone, Juliet Breese, Kate Davies, Katy Jackson, David Till, Bill Toop and Gary Wing
Original cover design by Oliver Design
Cover design by Andrew Magee Design Ltd
Cover photographs by Alamy/Life on White and Thinkstock/iStock/szefei

The publishers would like to thank the following:
Cambridge Publishing Management Limited

The authors and publishers would like to thank the following for permission to reproduce their photographs:

Alamy/A ROOM WITH VIEWS p138(1), Alamy/Action Plus Sports Images p130(diving), Alamy/Aflo Co. Ltd p130(6), Alamy/Vadym Andrushschenko p29(tl,1), Alamy/Bailey-Cooper Photography p31(pasta), Alamy/Richard Becker p65(bl), Alamy/Steve Bloom Images p146(bcl, tl),149(tl), Alamy/Bon Appetit p138(4/ice cream), Alamy/Todor Boyajiev pp146(bm),149(tcl), Alamy/Nancy Camel p66(cmll), Alamy/Cultura Creative p87(tl), Alamy/Andrew Darrington p65(bcl), Alamy/David Edsam p21(3), Alamy/Eureka p72(4), Alamy/even images p47(1), Alamy/foodfolio pp31(cakes, meat, cheese), 34(melon, cake),36(cake),39,47(cheese),76(2), Alamy/Richard Gleed p31(biscuits),Alamy/Tim Graham p79, Alamy/Robert Harding Picture Library Ltd p57(br), Alamy/Esa Hitula p138(basketball hoop), Alamy/incamerastock p31(bread), Alamy/James Jackson p112(4), Alamy/Juniors Bildarchiv GmbH p155, Alamy/julian marshall p21(2), Alamy/Mart of Images p87(tm), Alamy/Nordicphotos p66(bcr), Alamy/CHRISTINE OSBORNE PICTURES p36(pyramids), Alamy/AGUILAR PATRICE p20(tmll, 2, 4), Alamy/photonic 5 p31(butter), Alamy/PHOTOTAKE Inc p57(bmr), Alamy/Nicholas Pitt p126(tr), Alamy/Profimedia.CZ a.s. p153(tcr), Alamy/Mervyn Rees p127(c, cr),130(flag),131, Alamy/Shepic p138(walking), Alamy/South West Images Scotland p13(3), Alamy/Jack Sullivan p127(br), Alamy/Superstock p31(sweets), Alamy/Francis Vachon p130(3), Alamy/Westend61 GmbH pp65(cmll),118, Alamy/Gary Wilkinson p47(2); **Bananastock** pp34(french fries),138(2); **Brand X** p59; **Comstock** pp29(6), 47(3); **Corbis**/Bettman pp57(cmr, cr), 72(3), Corbis/Jonathan Blair p146(bmr),149(bl), Corbis/Daniel J. Cox p67(tl),70(panda), Corbis/Malcolm Fife p123, Corbis/Gavriel Jecan p112(1), Corbis/Oliver Lassen p29(3), Corbis/Raimund Linke p66(bcmll), Corbis/David Madison p130(tl), Corbis/Wally McNamee p129, Corbis/Ocean/176 p57(tcmr), Corbis/Reuters p20(5), Corbis/Dale Spartas p72(1), Corbis/Jim Sugar pp16,19(x3), Corbis/Adrianna Williams p21(1); **FLPA**/Andrew Parkinson p66(cr), FLPA/Jurgen & Christine Sohns pp67(br),70(giraffe),76(4), FLPA/Winifried Wisniewski p149(cl); **John Foxx Images** pp13(2),70(elephant),146(bmll); **Getty Images** pp29(2), 31(cereal, fish, milk), 34(pizza, banana),58 ,65(tl), 76(1), Getty Images/Al Bello p13(4), Getty Images/C Squared Studios pp31(rice, oils, fruit, vegetables), 36(fruit salad),84,112(2),138 (3), Getty Images/Caiaimage/Sam Edwards pp150,153(tr), Getty Images/Peter Dazeley p29(5), Getty Images/Jody Dole p138(4), Getty Images/Sylvain Grandadam p20(tl,1), Getty Images/James Gritz p78, Getty Images/Darrell Gulin p13(1), Getty Images/iStockphoto/Thinkstock/Jeff Huting pp50,142(br),143, Getty Images/iStockphoto/Thinkstock/Shane Maritch p13(tcr), Getty Images/iStockphoto/thumb p43, Getty Images/J&L Images p130(cycling), Getty Images/Keystone pp95, 98(tr), Getty Images/LWA p47(4),

Getty Images/Clive Mason p130(5), Getty Images/Wil Meinderts/Buiten-beeld/Minden Pictures p66(br), Getty Images/Mint Images/Frans Lantin p70(zebra), Getty Images/Bele Olmez p20(3), Getty Images/Photodisc p31(eggs), Getty Images/Peter Pinnock p112(5), Getty Images/Popperfoto pp98(cr),126(c), Getty Images/Bob Thomas/Popperfoto p126(br), Getty Images/Jim Reed p104, Getty Images/subjug p32, Getty Images/Bob Thomas p130(medallists); **Mary Evans Picture Library**/Illustrated London News Ltd p92(bcr); **Nature Picture Library**/Kim Taylor p65(tcl); **Photoalto** p34(tomato); **Photodisc** pp71, 72(2, 5), 76(3),112(6),146(bml, bmrr), Photodisc/Getty Images p31(water); **Press Association Images** p127(tr), Press Association Images/Empics pp130(1, 2, 4),133; **Rex Shutterstock**/FLPA p146(br), Rex Shutterstock/imageBROKER p149(bcl), Rex Shutterstock/Nature Picture Library p66(bmll); Science **Photo Library** p57(tmr); **Science and Society Picture Library**/Science Museum p57(tr, bcr), 92(tcr); **Thinkstock**/8thCreator p25, Thinkstock/iStock/anopdesignstock p36(tennis racquet), Thinkstock/iStock/antomanio pp51,142(cl), Thinkstock/iStock/HandmadePictures pp134,135, Thinkstock/kimkole p24, Thinkstock/Stockbyte p85, Thinkstock/Thomas Northcut p29(4), Thinkstock/Zoonar/J. Wachala p11; **Topfoto** pp93, 94.

The authors and publishers are grateful for permission to reprint the following copyright material:
Page 23: Martin Honeysett *When there's a Fire in the Jungle* from *Animal Nonsense Rhymes* (Egmont UK Ltd, London, 1984), © Martin Honeysett 1984, reprinted by permission of the publisher.
Page 23: Julie Edwards *The Sun* taken from *My Blue Poetry Book* edited by Moira Andrew (Macmillan Education, 1988).
Pages 24–5: Extract from *Clever Polly and the Stupid Wolf* by Catherine Storr (Faber and Faber, 1955), © Catherine Storr 1955, reprinted by permission of the publisher.
Page 39: Extracts from *The Guinness Book of World Records (2004)*, reprinted by permission of the publisher.
Pages 42–3: Extract from *Journey to Jo'burg* by Beverley Naidoo (Puffin Books, 1996), © Beverley Naidoo 1996, reprinted by permission of The Agency (London) Ltd.
Page 49: Adapted extracts from *Soraya's blanket* from *Junior Assembly Book* by Doreen Vause and Liz Beaumont (Macdonald Educational, 1989).
Page 65: Extract from *Ants and their Nest* by Christine Butterworth (Macmillan Education, 1988), © Christine Butterworth 1988, reprinted by permission of the author.
Page 73: Tony Mitton *Teaser* and *Undersea Tea* both © Tony Mitton 2000, first published in *The Works* by Paul Cookson (Macmillan Children's Books, 2000), reprinted by permission of David Higham Associates Limited.
Page 74: Robin Mellor *Lions* taken from *Reading Workshop 2* (Stanley Thornes Publishers Ltd, 1996).
Page 75: Spike Milligan *The Veggy Lion* © Spike Milligan Productions 1981, from *Unspun Socks from a Chicken's Laundry* (Michael Joseph, 1987), reprinted by permission of Spike Milligan Productions.
Page 99: Eric Finney *Thank You Letter* © Eric Finney 2000, first published in *Good Night, Sleep Tight* by Ivan and Mal Jones (Scholastic Press, 2000), reprinted by permission of the author.
Page 107: Extract from *Cambridge Primary Language Level 3 Study Skills* by Barbara Benson, Charles Cuff and Pauline Elkin (Cambridge University Press, 1984), reprinted by permission of the publisher and Charles Cuff.
Page 115: Mike Jubb *Wind* © Mike Jubb 2000, from *Poetry Works Book 2* (Folens, 2000), reprinted by permission of the author.
Pages 134–5: Extract from *A Martian in the Supermarket* by Penelope Lively (Hodder Children's Books, 2002), reprinted by permission of David Higham Associates Limited.
Page 151: Ray Mather *Remember Me?* taken from *Caribbean Junior Reader 5* (Ginn Publishers, 1994).
Page 157: John Cotton *The World with its Countries* © John Cotton, reprinted by permission of Peggy Cotton.

These materials may contain links for third party websites. We have no control over, and are not responsible for, the contents of such third party websites. Please use care when accessing them.

Printed and bound by CPI Group (UK) Ltd, Croydon, CR0 4YY
POD 2025